SOCIOCULTURAL PSYCHOLOGY AND REGULATORY PROCESSES IN LEARNING ACTIVITY

Written by educational researchers and professionals working with children and adolescents in and out of school, this book shows how self-regulation involves more than an isolated individual's ability to control their thoughts and feelings, particularly in learning environments. By using Vygotsky's cultural-historical psychological theory, the authors provide a unique set of four analytical lenses for a better understanding of how self-regulation, co-regulation, and other-regulation function as a system of regulatory processes. These lenses move beyond a focus on solitary individuals, who self-regulate behavior, to center on individuals as relational, agential, and contextually situated. As agents, teachers, mentors, and their students build their learning contexts and are influenced by these self-engineered contexts. This is a dynamic perspective of a social context and underlies the view that regulatory processes are an integral part of a functional system for learning.

LYNDA D. STONE is Professor of Child and Adolescent Development at California State University, Sacramento, USA where she has received awards for Outstanding Teaching and Community Service. Her research examines teaching–learning practices, with attention to learners from nondominant communities.

TABITHA HART is Associate Professor of Communication Studies at San José State University, USA. Her research areas include speech codes theory, ethnography of communication, and technology-mediated communication.

SOCIOCULTURAL PSYCHOLOGY AND REGULATORY PROCESSES IN LEARNING ACTIVITY

Contributions of Cultural-Historical Psychological Theory

LYNDA D. STONE

California State University, Sacramento

TABITHA HART

San José State University

CAMBRIDGE
UNIVERSITY PRESS

CAMBRIDGE
UNIVERSITY PRESS

University Printing House, Cambridge CB2 8BS, United Kingdom

One Liberty Plaza, 20th Floor, New York, NY 10006, USA

477 Williamstown Road, Port Melbourne, VIC 3207, Australia

314–321, 3rd Floor, Plot 3, Splendor Forum, Jasola District Centre,
New Delhi – 110025, India

79 Anson Road, #06–04/06, Singapore 079906

Cambridge University Press is part of the University of Cambridge.

It furthers the University's mission by disseminating knowledge in the pursuit of
education, learning, and research at the highest international levels of excellence.

www.cambridge.org
Information on this title: www.cambridge.org/9781107105034
DOI: 10.1017/9781316225226

First published 2019

Printed in the United Kingdom by TJ International Ltd, Padstow Cornwall

A catalogue record for this publication is available from the British Library.

ISBN 978-1-107-10503-4 Hardback

This book is dedicated to my husband Jim for his ongoing help and kind patience. It is also dedicated to all of the children, mentors, and teachers who welcomed me into their lives and their learning settings.

Lynda D. Stone

Contents

Figures

Transcription Excerpts

Foreword

Childhood as a Social Category: Moving from Disposability to Actively Co-constructing the World

At the time of writing, in the month of December, in 2018, at least two migrant children – Jakelin Ameí Rosmery Caal Maquin and Felipe Gomez Alonzo – died while in US custody. In that year, youth care workers at government-contracted shelters for migrant children were charged with the sexual assault of children in their care (Haag, 2018). Laws, policies, and practices enable children to be treated as disposable. At this time in US history, children, especially working-class and working-poor children of color, are often viewed as dispensable. And, if these children are expendable, then many children and youth can also be viewed similarly due to their shared subordinated social category: childhood. Indeed, even when middle-class youth rise up and ask decision makers to treat them with inherent worth and dignity, as was the case after the massacre at Marjory Stoneman Douglas High School in Parkland, Florida, they are mocked and regarded as patsies, or even paid crisis actors (Alter, 2018; Wootson, 2018).

To treat children as disposable also requires viewing them as less capable and as *becoming* rather than as already *being* complete persons in themselves. Relatedly, their individual and collective agency is questioned (Langhout & Thomas, 2010). I have found evidence of this disparaging social labeling in my research, where elementary school–aged Latinx children were viewed as incapable when they called attention to classism and racism and wished to document their sense of collective agency and nonviolent direct action against it in a school-based mural (Kohfeldt, Bowen, & Langhout, 2016).

Although children's abilities are often questioned, history documents their individual and collective agency. Two US-based examples are the Children's Crusade and the 1899 New York newsboys strike. With respect to the Children's Crusade, thousands of Black children – some as young as seven years old – marched for several days for their civil rights in Birmingham, Alabama in 1963. Most of the children were subjected to police brutality and approximately 2,500 of them were arrested for their nonviolent direct action. The Children's Crusade is now viewed as a turning point for civil rights legislation, in that it was a crucial moment for President Kennedy, who had remained largely silent regarding civil rights until this show of collective agency (Children's Crusade, n.d.; Gilmore, 2014).

The 1899 New York newsboys strike lasted two weeks (Campbell Bartoletti, 1999). At this time, orphaned and unhoused children sold newspapers across the United States. Some newsboys were as young as eight years old. In New York, Pulitzer and Hearst owned the two main papers and raised the price for the papers to be bought by the newsboys but not the price for the newsboys to sell the papers. The newsboys found this model financially unsustainable, especially since Pulitzer and Hearst refused to buy back unsold papers. As a result, the newsboys called for a strike and more than 7,000 newsboys marched through the city, halting traffic. Owing to the strike, newspaper sales plummeted. Pulitzer and Hearst agreed to buy back unsold papers and the direct action inspired other newsboys strikes in Montana and Kentucky (Campbell Bartoletti, 1999).

The social category of childhood, and subsequent views of their individual and collective agency (or lack thereof), does not happen in a vacuum. Indeed, social constructions, cultural regularities, historical context and moment, and policies, practices, and procedures matter, to name only a few systems. Yet, in psychology and education, we sometimes ignore how these larger structures inform human behavior and learning. We do this at our own peril, for, when we ignore these structures, we create ahistorical, asocial, and acultural theory and analysis (Sarason, 1981).

I first met Professor Lynda D. Stone more than ten years ago, when I was a new partner in UC Links, a network of after-school programs that began in California and is now worldwide. As a youth participatory action researcher and social-community psychologist, I saw the differences between my paradigm and that of many others in the network. It was Lynda who created a bridge to show me the similarities between my programmatic research and what was happening at the prolific 5th Dimension sites that comprised a large part of the network at that time. What I most appreciate about the work that Lynda presents in this book is the bridging that she continues to do.

Lynda encourages us to engage in analysis from a framework that is broader than one person or even a dyad. She wants us to consider not only student–teacher interactions, or even student–student interactions, but also the social, relational, and contextual dimensions that shape what happens in any setting, including a learning space. Specifically, she demands that we consider children as active co-constructors and co-regulators of any space that they inhabit. In other words, through their agency and actions, they co-configure much of the world. This, however, is the paradox: although children have agency, they also experience tremendous levels of subordination, given the current social construction of the category of childhood in the United States. Moreover, if children also inhabit other subordinated social categories related to race, ethnicity, citizenship status, social class, sexuality, and so on, then they are even more inhibited in exercising their agency.

Lynda does not shy away from this paradox. Instead, she focuses on the learning environment, which is an especially challenging and poignant choice given that children in these settings are often positioned as receivers who are being regulated. Indeed, it is rare that they are conceptualized as active co-constructors and co-regulators of learning and of the cultural practices of the setting. It is even more rare for them to be seen as contributors to the social order, moral order, and relational habitus (i.e., "an ecological ensemble of relations including self, tools, tasks, and others that is intersubjectively constructed and sustained over time in formal and informal learning communities" [Stone, Underwood, & Hotchkiss, 2012, p. 66]). Through rich examples, however, Lynda demonstrates co-regulation and co-construction not only in "alternative" learning environments but also in more conventional ones, demonstrating how children co-construct these larger systems.

Through her theoretical and analytical lens, Lynda draws our attention to the social, relational, and contextual dimensions of these learning environments by carefully pointing out the traces of them in speech, intonation, mood, and more. Much like the work of anthropologist Jean Briggs, Lynda brings us in close so we can better glimpse the bigger picture. Through her approach, we see that the social and moral order is both historical and emerging, yet never completely fixed or determined, just as we see how mood is relational and moves across time and space.

At this historical moment especially, where children are seemingly viewed as disposable know-nothings, the perspective Lynda offers is a radical and hopeful one. It is radical to listen carefully to elementary school–aged children, to take them seriously, and to document the ways in which they co-construct the world. It is courageously hopeful to see them as people who are currently helping to construct an emerging social and moral order within a specific historical context. Finally, it is generous for Lynda to provide tools for others to follow this path of seeing the bigger picture within everyday interactions and to understand how tone, intonation, mood, and more are traces of social, relational, and contextual dimensions that demonstrate the history and emergence of the social and moral order.

In community,

REGINA DAY LANGHOUT, PH.D.
Professor of Psychology
University of California, Santa Cruz

Acknowledgments

The key to success for individuals and communities emerges from our practices, from our relationship to family, friends, and colleagues within these practices, and from the ever flowing and changing ideas, concepts, and cultural toolkits we create with others through our practices. In my case, I collaborated with a wonderful colleague, Tabitha Hart, to write this book, and, yes, it is a book with limitations but with the genuine hope of contributing to conceptual frames for researching regulatory processes during learning practices in social contexts. Our hope is that these analytical frames can also offer ideas or tools for creating the very best learning arenas for children or adults to become active agents in the construction of their learning contexts and in the ways they regulate their behaviors for thinking, feeling, being, and doing.

My journey in this process began when, as a classroom teacher, I decided to enroll in a University of California, Los Angeles (UCLA) doctoral program in education. This program changed my knowledge and ideas, my perspective on the world, and my sense of self by making it possible for me to take an interdisciplinary approach to understanding human learning and development. These changes were beautifully influenced by Professor Kris Gutierrez, my young UCLA mentor and advisor, who invited me to join in her own intellectual pursuits by accompanying her to the Laboratory of Comparative Human Cognition (LCHC) at University of California, San Diego so that we could meet Michael Cole, his colleagues, and his students. This magical meeting place is one of research, novel ideas, and, yes, care: care for children, care for families, and care for our communities. Along with Kris, I continued going to LCHC's meetings for more than three years. During this time, I learned how theory, research, and everyday practices can be woven together in practical ways to make a difference in the world. I have continued in a relationship with LCHC for more than twenty years, first as a UCLA postdoctoral fellow who helped to create and run a unique after-school program based on an approach developed by Michael Cole and his colleagues, the Fifth Dimension (5thD). Later, as a professor, I developed a local 5thD after-school site in northern California. The researchers and scholars in all of my experiences at UCLA, LCHC, and, later, the University of California's UC Links after-school community have influenced this book, influences for which I am deeply grateful.

My academic and research experiences lead me to reflect on my own teaching and, I am proud to say, my many successes with children. These successes are related to this book, in that the ways I helped children, without realizing it, were related to behavior regulation. To share an example, I describe Mustafa; he is a smiling third grader with big brown eyes who simply did not know how to "behave" in classroom settings. He often danced quickly across the classroom while swinging his arms in a joyful manner and, at other times, in playful ways, he would lose his focus on the tasks at hand – not at all controlling his behavior appropriate to classroom settings. At least that is what one of my colleagues thought. We co-taught together but in different classrooms and, as a consequence, Mustafa experienced different instructional practices. By mid-year, because of Mustafa's behavior, my colleague referred him to what was then called a "special education" program. Fortunately, Mustafa was not placed in this program. And, by the year's end, my colleague said to me, "You've worked wonders with him!" At the time, I did not think I had worked wonders. Rather, I thought he was just a child, a charming one at that, who needed help in learning how to participate in a classroom. I also knew that the other children had to "see" themselves in a positive, helpful, and playful relationship with Mustafa. This relationship was also one that had to be created among all of the children – it was a kind of moral understanding about how to regulate behaviors by helping each other succeed with all of their academic tasks. And, *over time*, I helped these children, along with Mustafa, come to this understanding. At the time, did I think of it as practical–moral ways of regulating behavior in a learning setting? Nope. That understanding, that theoretical knowledge, was to come later, after I had analyzed two of my video ethnographies of formal and informal learning contexts. But, once I was able to "see" this form of knowledge and how it shaped engagement, I realized it was characteristic of all learning contexts – work, school, and homes.

Over time, I came to see that I had used my own understandings of what children needed from their teachers or mentors to learn how to regulate their behavior in academic contexts. These understandings represented my own informal theories about teaching and learning. Had these informal theories been transformed through research into more formally articulated and socially shared theories, they may have offered others (including myself) a set of reflective tools for creating optimal learning environments in an explicit and, perhaps, more systematic approach. The analytical frames detailed in this book offer a set of tools for such an approach. They were constructed by paying close attention to learning contexts and how these contexts are created from transactions between individuals and their mentors or teachers or parents – transactions that always involve varying forms of behavior regulation.

My formal investigations into regulatory behaviors in learning situations were not done as an individual process. Three of the chapters in this book were adapted from previously published research articles and were written in collaboration with my colleagues and, at times, with my students. The chapter on the relational habitus, published in *Human Development*, includes contributions from my colleague Dr. Charles Underwood and a graduate student, Jacqueline Hotchkiss. The chapter on practical-moral knowledge was published in *Mind, Culture and Activity* and included contributions from an undergraduate student, Madeleine Kerrick, and a graduate student, Rita Stoeckl. The chapter on contextual mood was published in *Learning, Culture and Social Interaction* and genuinely co-authored by my colleague Professor Gregory Thompson. The thoughtful comments from the editors in each of the journals and from the editors at Cambridge University Press also contributed to this book. The chapter on identities of competency represented two years of analyses with my colleague Professor Tabitha Hart. Finally, I am especially grateful for the insightful comments and feedback from my colleagues Professor Basia Ellis and Provost Regina Day Langhout.

LYNDA STONE

My path toward working on this book began when I was an undergraduate student majoring in Communication at the University of California, San Diego. There, I had the great opportunity to study and work with Dr. Olga Vásquez on her after-school project La Clase Mágica. It was Dr. Vásquez who introduced me to a whole host of theoretical, methodological, and practical tools that would become the foundation of my future academic career, including how to structure a qualitative research project, from mindfully engaging in participant observation, to writing ethnographic fieldnotes, to interpreting data, and then presenting these interpretations in a conference setting. Thank you so much Olga – I am very grateful to have had you as my teacher.

Fortuitously, it was working with Dr. Vásquez that brought me to Lynda. In 2002, I was a new M.A. student at California State University, Sacramento (CSUS). Based on my prior experience working with Dr. Vásquez and La Clase Mágica, Lynda invited me to join the research team for her own 5thD after-school site. This was an incredible stroke of fortune and it turned out to inform and shape my entire academic career. It was Lynda who taught me how to design and execute a multisited, qualitative research project, including how to write a proposal, navigate a fieldsite, record and transcribe data, use discourse analytic methods to interpret data, and write up research reports. It was also Lynda who cheered me on in pursuing a Ph.D. and ultimately becoming a professor in the CSU system myself. Along the way, Lynda has been my role model for what it means to be a good academic, public servant, colleague, and university-level teacher. Thank you so much Lynda – you have indelibly shaped my career and my life. I am so grateful for your generous mentorship and friendship all along the way.

TABITHA HART

Transcription Conventions

Layout	Speakers are indicated by initial letters of name or name. Their utterances and paralinguistic data are numbered consecutively.
-	A hyphen shown at the end of talk indicates incomplete utterances.
::	Colons represent elongated speech or a stretched sound.
° °	Utterances between degree symbols indicate whispered or quiet speech in relation to surrounding utterances.
=	The equal sign represents latched speech, a continuation of talk, useful when a speaker (interlocutor) is interrupted.
(1.0)	A number inside brackets denotes a timed pause in seconds. This is a pause long enough to time and subsequently shown in transcription.
.	One period represents a perceptible pause in talk, thereafter longer pauses are represented by: (.) = 0.4 seconds (..) = 0.6 seconds (. . .) = 0.8 seconds
↑	An upward arrow means there is a rise in intonation.
↓	A downward arrow means there is a drop in intonation.
→	An arrow like this denotes a particular sentence of interest to the analyst.
[	Square brackets denote a point where overlapping speech is initiated.
> <	Arrows surrounding talk show that the pace of the speech has quickened.
< >	Arrows in this direction show that the pace of the speech has slowed down.
( )	Where there is space between brackets, it denotes that the words spoken here were too unclear to transcribe or could not be heard.
(( ))	Where double italic parentheses appear with a description inserted denotes some contextual information – paralinguistic *data* such as gestures, eye gaze, body positioning, and so on.
Under	When a word or part of a word is underlined, it denotes a rise in volume or emphasis.
CAPITALS	Where capital letters appear, it denotes that something was said loudly or even shouted.
(h)	When an 'h' appears in parentheses, it means that there was laughter within the talk – these h's can be repeated to indicate longer periods of laughter, e.g., hhhhhh.

Introduction

What determines our judgment, our concepts, and reactions, is not
what one man is doing now, an individual action, but the whole hurly-
burly of human actions, the background against which we see an action.

Wittgenstein (1981)

Our worlds – including our learning contexts – are created, maintained,
and transformed through our engagement with others. This is a social,
relational, agentive, creative, and sustained process of "context using and
context creating." We create these contexts (these lived worlds) by controlling and directing our thoughts, feelings, desires, actions, and interactions with social others to make meaning, to figure out problems, to
construct knowledge, and to inhabit diverse social identities. Through
this process, we gain voluntary control over our social, psychological,
and practical behaviors, which is generally referred to as self-regulated
behavior or self-regulated learning. The emphasis on "self" is no accident,
as it reflects dominant worldviews of human development as an individual
and mental process (Shweder, 1991). This is a one-sided, mentalist view of
human development and it is changing. At present, across social sciences,
a relational view of human development is taking hold because of
Vygotsky's (1981, 1934/1986) radical cultural-historical theory of psychological development and related social and cultural theories (Barad, 2007;
Dewey, 1929/1958; Gibson, 1969, 1986; Mead, 1934/1962; Shotter, 2016).
The relational view conceptualizes the human mind as emerging from
meaning-making processes situated in social contexts, mediated by cultural
artifacts and sign systems, and distributed across individuals, tools, tasks,
space, and time. The shift toward this relational view of mind requires an
alternative approach to regulatory processes – an approach that sees human
development as a social, relational, and cultural process in which individuals and their communities co-develop, effectively transforming the paths
toward competent social and psychological selves.

This book builds on Vygotsky's work and the work of other closely related social and cultural theorists (e.g., Bourdieu, 1980, 1985; Cole, 1996; Engeström, 1999; Miller & Goodnow, 1995; Kockelman, 2006; Shotter, 1993; Valsiner, 2001; Wertsch, 1985, 1991) to broaden contemporary views of behavioral regulation. Specifically, we offer a novel approach to behavioral regulation that helps explain how ways of controlling, directing, and constructing complex cognitive behaviors emerge from relational and agential processes of engagement that are continuously interwoven with a community's cultural and semiotic resources, including tools and signs, norms, values, expectations, and moral ethos. To do this, we draw on sociocultural theories to develop four alternate, sociocultural frames intended to illuminate how social contexts and learning processes (and/or developmental processes) are interrelated. These new frames are designed to bring into focus how engagement in *all* forms of behavioral regulation (self-, co-, and other-) and socially shared regulatory processes function together as relational parts of a whole system for gaining, maintaining, and displaying competencies in the lived world. This entanglement of regulatory processes is an integral part of social, individual, contextual, and instrumental (mediational) aspects of controlling and directing ways of thinking, feeling, and doing. Of course, from this perspective, self-regulated behavior plays an important part in the process that Vygotsky (1978) calls "the internalization of higher psychological processes" by individuals (p. 52). Processes of internalization accomplished by individuals suggest that self-regulation is implicated in all forms of behavioral regulation; simultaneously, these processes are always situated in the sociocultural world. This points to why the central concern of our argument is not simply the self-regulatory processes of individuals. Rather, we focus on behavioral regulation as a whole system of regulatory processes that constitute the relational and socioculturally situated ways active agents continuously co-construct and change psychological phenomena in activities with others.

The social and cultural processes that give rise to competencies with regulatory processes reflect Vygotsky's (1934/1987) claim that learners "with collaboration, direction, or some kind of help ... [are] always able to do more and solve more difficult tasks" than they can do "independently" (p. 209). Here, Vygotsky's use of the term "independently" is referring to individual development as the primary goal of interacting with others or, in his words, "man mastering processes of his own behavior" through self-regulation of reasoning, thinking, and feeling (Vygotsky, 1987, pp. 242–243). Yet the very essence of this process involves the social genesis of voluntary control over culturally organized mental functions, such as deliberately remembering or deliberately controlling attention. Fundamental to this process is a recursive and bidirectional relationship between individuals and their cultural milieus, a relationship in which they develop together. This co-evolving and bidirectional relationship also suggests why competencies with all forms of behavioral regulation are necessary for social and psychological development.

Of course, human development necessarily requires individuals to learn how to self-regulate or master their own thinking, feelings, and actions in the midst of ongoing activities (Vygotsky, 1978). But, facility with self-regulation also requires individuals to master ways of interacting with others to gain, maintain, and develop this competency, which is part of an ever-changing "formative or developmental process" involving a system of regulatory behaviors (Shotter, 1993). For example, during literacy learning, the entanglement of regulatory processes can be very complex. Consider a lesson on poetry where the teacher's goal is to help children learn how to recognize poetic elements and how to use these elements to create their own poems through collaborative large- and small-group activities. In such an activity, children can be seen self-regulating their attention toward the teacher's explanations. This would also involve learning how to focus (regulate) attention on particular aspects of a poem. Engagement in this form of self-regulation might also be utilized to understand different forms of texts – for example, expository or persuasive writing. In the same poetry activity, self-regulation may simultaneously become entangled with co-regulation where learners focus their actions and interactions on collaboratively accomplishing the same goal. Further, these co-regulatory processes may occur along with other-regulation where the teacher controls the learners' actions through explicit directives that lead learners to work independently or collaboratively. Later, children may revoice the teacher's directives as a strategy to self-regulate their own behaviors. Similarly, in small-group learning, children can revoice strategies as a way of assisting one another to achieve a shared or individual goal. In these and other complex ways of learning, regulatory processes become an integral part of transforming thought, feelings, and actions. Accordingly, aptitudes for controlling and directing psychological and pragmatic behaviors necessarily involve all forms of regulatory behaviors (self-, co-, other-) to coordinate and collaborate on actions and interactions in the "whole hurly-burly of human actions."

In everyday activities, interactions with others always necessitate facility with *a repertoire of ways to regulate behaviors*. This repertoire is an essential part of in situ arrangements that foster developmental processes. Shotter (2016) refers to these developmental processes as "relational becomings" in that our competencies with regulatory processes are always connected to our social and material world and always part of an "unbounded" or "incomplete" process open to further development (p. 27). The development of behavioral repertories for controlling and directing thinking, feeling, and volitional inclinations consistently emerges and becomes elaborated from engaging in meaning-making with social others. It is in this relational process of becoming psychologically and socially competent that we learn to regulate our behaviors with others to exploit, create, discover, and potentially change a myriad of semiotic/contextual resources, including communicative strategies, social rules/values, symbolic and material tools, and our local community's moral ethos or guide for "the right way" to interact with others. In this way, individual learning and development are constitutively interwoven with social and cultural development.

With the goal of contributing to understanding these relational processes of learning and development, this book presents a view of behavioral regulation that is grounded in cultural psychology (Cole, 1996; Ellis & Stam, 2015; Leont'ev, 1981; Vygotsky, 1978; Engeström, 1999). Our approach offers analytical frames that make it possible to understand more deeply how we regulate our behaviors in relation to our lived worlds. It also offers a means to reveal how actions and interactions are coordinated through flowing, emerging, and evolving configurations of self-, other-, co-, and socially shared regulatory processes in habitual and creative ways. Our view of behavioral regulation as part of a relational process of human development changes the focus from the solitary individual to the relational ways in which agentive individuals collaborate and coordinate their actions and interactions, utilizing all forms of regulatory processes to become competent members of their communities.

Self-Regulation in Learning Communities: A Concept in Transition

Self-controlled and self-directed actions and interactions across learning settings, both in and out of school, have traditionally been studied as originating from individuals' perceptions, thoughts, attitudes, and feelings about their past experiences (Panadero, 2017). These psychological responses to prior experience are assumed to influence individuals' capacities to self-regulate their cognitive, emotional, and volitional behaviors.

In other words, this view emphasizes the role of the individual in initiating, adapting, and maintaining their thoughts, feelings, and pragmatic behaviors in relation to ongoing engagement in the world (Forgas, Baumeister, & Tice, 2009; Schunk & Zimmerman, 2006). With this explicit focus on the developmental outcomes of autonomous and isolated individuals, it is no wonder that self-regulation, animated by the emphasis on "self," became the cynosure for understanding how individuals construct knowledge to develop academic, psychological, and real-world competencies. This historical focus in psychological research on individuals and how they self-regulate has resulted in a systematic neglect of the relational, social, material, and contextual dimensions of learning. Yet these neglected aspects of the lived world are the very resources we use and the very resources we create to control and direct our thoughts, feelings, actions, and desires. Further, the emphasis on self-regulation elides how agentive individuals co-inhabit and co-create learning contexts through a shifting repertoire of regulatory processes that, over time, form the basis for collaboratively built social contexts, which orient learners to social others, the unfolding meanings of their tasks, and a host of artifacts (tools/ideas) that can be used in problem-solving or cognitive activities. In other words, psychological approaches to behavioral regulation lack the theoretical and conceptual means to account for the social, relational, and contextual dimensions that are an essential part of social selves and learning activities.

Self-Regulation in Social Contexts

Over the last twenty years or so, social scientists have begun to move beyond the individual to consider the role of the social context in shaping regulatory processes, particularly in educational research. These studies tend to conceptualize self-regulation as embedded in and influenced by learning contexts (Allal, 2011; Panadero & Järvelä, 2015). Here, context is often framed as a cuing mechanism for the development of self-regulation. In other words, learners use contextual cues to regulate their engagement in learning as a fundamentally self-organized process of control, volition, and adaptation. Yet, time and again, researchers assume that it is the autonomous individual who is responsible for directing, controlling, and maintaining motivational inclinations to self-regulate thinking and feeling strategies used to monitor, plan, and control engagement in learning tasks (Boekaerts, 2001; Martinek, Hofmann, & Kipman, 2016; Rief, 2007). The contextual influences used by learners are viewed as emerging from instructional or mentoring approaches found in formal or informal learning activities (Fuhs, Farrran, & Nesbitt, 2013; de Bruin & van Gog, 2012). That is, learning contexts preexist to some degree in that they are created for learners by teachers or mentors. Although this view recognizes the influences of the context, it obscures whatever contributions learners make to the construction of local contexts as they negotiate the uncertainties, ambiguities, and conflicts that are characteristic of learning activities.

Even with the acknowledgment of the social world, the body of work that focuses on individuals offers only limited theoretical accounts of the interrelationship of regulatory processes with the social, relational, and contextual aspects of the lived world (for exceptions, see Iiskala et al., 2011; Hadwin & Oshige, 2011). Why is this the case? The newer views of regulatory processes as embedded in social contexts and the more mainstream psychological approaches share a worldview in which individuals and their thinking are "bounded entities" separate from the lived world (Shotter, 2014). Put simply, the thoughts and ideas that influence engagement in regulatory processes are "hidden within the heads of individuals" even if cued or supported by social contexts (Shotter, 2014, p. 1). We posit that the separation of the cultural world from individual development is no longer tenable given our growing understandings of human development as emerging from complex, dynamic, and constantly evolving transactions between agential individuals and their sociocultural contexts.

From Self-Regulation to a Dynamic Interplay of Regulatory Processes

The ascendance of sociocultural theories of human learning and development has led to a profound conceptual shift in how we view individuals and their cultural contexts (Kirschner & Martin, 2010). No longer separated from the social milieu, individuals are enmeshed in a relational entanglement with their social and material worlds, the nature of which can be traced to Vygotsky's widely acknowledged claim that mental functioning, including cognitive and emotional-volitional aspects, originates in a system of social processes and relationships. Vygotsky summarized this relational view in his general genetic law of cultural development:

> Any function in the child's cultural development appears twice, or on two planes. First it appears on the social plane, and then on the psychological plane. First it appears between people as an interpsychological category, and then within the child as an intrapsychological category. This is equally true with regard to voluntary [qua regulated] attention, logical memory, the formation of concepts, and the development of volition [qua motivation] ... it goes

without saying that internalization transforms the process itself and changes its structure and functions. Social relations or relations among people genetically underlie all higher functions and their relationships. (Vygotsky, 1981, p. 163)

Vygotsky's unique perspective on regulatory processes is that the emergence, control, and direction of cognitive and emotional processes such as deliberate memory, selective attention, meaning-making perception, and volition (motivation) first appear between people and are later internalized (appropriated) by individuals. This means that the regulation of psychological behaviors is first socially constructed with others and later appropriated (creatively adapted) by individuals for their own purposes. As a consequence, the development of competencies with behavioral regulation emerges from socially organized learning activities where children (and adults) learn how, when, and where to control and direct their feelings, thoughts, ideas, actions, and desires or inclinations for active engagement with social others. This points to why behavioral regulation is an intellectual and social-emotional competency that emerges as individuals collaboratively engage in the continuously unfolding ambiguities and uncertainties of learning practices to make meaning with others. In effect, there is a fundamental relationship between regulatory processes and the complexity of meaning-making processes during learning.

Cultural Practices and Regulatory Processes

Interestingly, the same actions and social interactions used in behavioral regulation both exploit and create the learning *practices* of local communities. All practices emerge from and are created through the routine and valued activities of a local culture and thus provide repeated opportunities for individuals to learn how to take control and regulate their psychological and practical behaviors. Because of this, cultural practices – whether academic, work, or play – exert a significant role in helping learners decide when, how, and under what circumstances to regulate behavior. For example, cooking practices with children might include activities such as learning how to read and follow recipes; shop for ingredients; and use tools such as digital scales, mixers, blenders, or even rules of thumb. During cooking practices, learners may come to understand how to regulate their psychological and practical behaviors to achieve their culinary goals. These cooking practices will likely involve interactions with others (collaborators, mentors, parents, etc.) as well as the use of particular systems of knowledge and technologies.

This is why engagement in regulatory processes does not simply occur within the "heads of individuals" but rather in relationships with social others in the material and symbolic world. Likewise, these processes will also relate to the problems or tasks at hand as well as what tools are available. Through engagement in local learning practices, intellectual, social-emotional, and motivational changes will occur. Over time, these changes transform how learners regulate their thoughts, feelings, actions, and ways of being with others during routine learning practices. Understanding how these changes occur requires a more nuanced conceptualization of context and its role in social and relational processes of behavioral regulation.

The purpose of this book is to offer unique sociocultural frames to assist scholars, research practitioners, students, and educators in understanding the transactions that lead to regulatory actions by agential learners in social contexts. Our approach views behavioral regulation as shaped by an emergent relatedness arising from learners' orientation to others in their surroundings, to their tools, to their tasks, and to their active roles in the ongoing creation of the "the whole hurly-burly" of learning activities. An important part of this orientation to others is the enactment of agency in routine activity. In other words, the ways that participants in a practice actively control and direct (regulate) their behaviors to affect the world. Thus, fundamental to our approach is the idea that individuals are engaged in agential processes that unfold through alternate configurations of self-, other-, co-, and socially shared regulation situated in social-historical contexts. Following Karen Barad (2007), we see agency not as an individual "attribute but the ongoing reconfiguring of the world" (p. 141). From this perspective, agency is spontaneously emerging and relational and comes into existence through actions and interactions used to exert control over, and create, the social world. As learners and their peers, mentors, or teachers continually configure, reconfigure, and reinterpret their relationships to those around them, their tools, and their tasks, they creatively transform practice and build a cultural context. All of this hinges on learners' historical (over time) engagement in regulatory processes of doing, thinking, and being; thus, all participants in locally situated practices are involved in creating an ecological system of influences on regulatory processes.

To capture how regulatory processes emerge, each of the following chapters in this book offers a different analytical frame with which to view those complex transactions that give rise to regulatory actions. A brief description of each chapter follows.

In Chapter 1, we present an overview of Vygotsky's (1978) *cultural-historical activity theory* (CHAT), including an explanation of how regulatory processes arise from the routine practices of social life. As part of this overview, we provide an explicit definition of cultural practices. To elaborate how a practice perspective is beneficial for understanding behavioral regulation, we describe the basic elements of an activity theory framework as aspects of a social practice. This framework offers a useful model for conceptualizing and observing how social practices come into existence and create the contextual resources (e.g., cultural tools and sign systems or symbols) that influence behavioral regulation. We conclude this chapter with definitions of self-, other-, and co-regulation, which are used in all analyses of learning contexts.

In Chapter 2, we offer a conceptual frame referred to as the *relational habitus* (RH), which can be used to observe how meaning-making processes (intersubjectivity) are co-constructed over synchronic (interactional) and diachronic (historical) time. The relational habitus is an ecological ensemble of relations including self, tools, tasks, and others that is intersubjectively constructed and sustained over time in formal and informal learning communities (Stone, Underwood, & Hotchkiss, 2012). It explains how variances in the social organization of regulatory processes are related to learning arenas, the interactional contexts of these arenas, and movement in the social and psychological spaces of these arenas. As a tool used for observing behavioral regulation during meaning-making, the RH encompasses three interrelated aspects of intersubjectivity: (1) an orientation to others in cultural contexts, (2) mutual perspective-taking accomplished through communication, and (3) perspective-making emerging from the ongoing negotiation of ambiguities and uncertainties of learning. These three aspects of intersubjectivity explain how regulatory processes emerging from and changing through meaning-making involve both the agential actions of individuals and the situational structuring of these actions.

Engagement in regulatory processes involves enacting behaviors within an RH and this engagement reflects a moral responsiveness to others, to how tools are used, and to how tasks are to be accomplished. To better understand this moral responsiveness, in Chapter 3 we present a theoretical frame that describes the contextual construction of *practical-moral knowledge* (PMK). PMK can be used to understand the dynamic transactions between the historical construction of a social context and behavioral regulation. PMK, found in all formal and informal learning communities, is constructed and reconstructed from a continually emergent and shared semiotic (sign) system of rights, responsibilities, and duties that establishes legitimate actions and interactions for competent participation. It creates a *community ethos*, which is a sign system comprising two components: (1) *social order* or practical/implicit understandings of who does what, when, and where and (2) *moral order* or implicit understandings of what is desirable, preferred, good, and right for regulating engagement in learning activity (Stone, Kerrick, & Stoeckl, 2013). As a socially embedded contextual influence, PMK shapes how learners create meaning with others in relation to tools and tasks. In effect, PMK creates a community ethos involving a code of conduct for regulating behaviors, a code always under revision as learners and the community co-develop. One way of observing the emergence of regulatory processes in the dynamic relationship between learners and their local community is to consider how learners (and their mentors/teachers) use locally constructed PMK to guide engagement in processes of self-, other-, and co-regulation.

In Chapter 4, we suggest that competency be reimagined as a social identity. Social identities are inhabited or embodied representations (signs) of the values and statuses of a community. These identities can be explicit to the extent that they are defined by socially and historically shared agreements – for example, learner, mentor, researcher, or teacher. Social identities can also be implicit to the extent that they are recognized in a community of practice but not publicly articulated. An *identity of competency* is an example of an implicit form of social identity that is linked to a local community's values and expectations of how to be, act, or feel as a competent member. In learning settings, an identity of competency is implicitly valued and highly desired because it not only indicates a willingness to persist in complex learning but also brings recognition and status (rights/power) for regulating the behaviors of self and others. This form of identity comes into existence when learners regulate their behaviors to align with a (continually emerging) socially shared category for competency. Through this alignment, learners vie to inhabit an identity of competency by employing those psychological and pragmatic acts of behavioral regulation marked as competent.

Chapter 5 offers the concept of *contextual mood* to capture how emotional (affective) experiences are interwoven with cognitive engagement in learning practices, where feelings permeate actions and thoughts and emerge through The , a linguistic resource used during social interactions (Stone & Thompson, 2014). The creation of a contextual mood attunes learners to particular forms of behavioral regulation as learning activities unfold. We explain how a contextual mood prompts young learners to consider, utilize, and potentially contribute to a repertoire of strategies for regulating meaning-making behaviors during literacy learning.

The Conclusion provides an overview of our theoretical approach and details how each of the sociocultural lenses presented in this book offers reflective and analytical tools for better understanding behavioral regulation as a system of self-, other-, co-, and socially shared regulatory processes. Reconceptualizing competence as involving all forms of behavioral regulation moves us away from the dualisms characteristic of traditional psychological approaches that divide the self from culture and the individual from society. Our analytical lenses do not reject the importance of an individual's development of psychological and practical actions over time but rather reframe them as part of a relational process of agency in which the regulated actions and interactions used to enact and develop intellectual and social emotional competences are always part of the sociocultural world.

CHAPTER I

Cultural-Historical Psychological Theory

Cultural psychology is changing our understandings about regulatory processes by offering newer conceptualizations of human learning and development as profoundly cultural. From this conceptualization, the cognitive, emotional, and volitional dimensions of learning emerge through collaborative engagement in cultural practices and are therefore situated in the social and historical contexts of local communities. This is an ecological perspective that views individuals as "spontaneously responsive, moving, embodied, living beings immersed . . . [in] agential activity" shaped through meaning-making and emerging from an entangled relational process with others, mediational artifacts, and tasks (Shotter, 2014, p. 306; Stone et al., 2012). This perspective is often referred to as a sociocultural approach, which can be traced back to Vygotsky's (1978) cultural-historical psychological theory of human development. Despite some disagreement about the similarities and differences between sociocultural and cultural-historical theories, both are rooted in Vygotsky's dialectical view that human development emerges from a dynamic relation between individuals and their social world. This Vygotskian view sees learning and development as constructed through participation in cultural practices where semiotic systems (tools and signs) are used to self-, co-, and other-regulate psychological and practical behaviors. To refer to Vygotskian theory in this book, we use the following two terms interchangeably: *sociocultural* and, following Michael Cole (2005), *cultural-historical activity theory*, or CHAT, a blend of terms proposed by Vygotsky (1978) and his colleagues (Leont'ev, 1981; Luria, 1928).

Fundamental Principles of Human Development

The Laboratory of Comparative Human Cognition or LCHC (2010) documented five fundamental principles of human development that characterize the CHAT approach. We offer the following adaptations and expansions of these principles to reflect their relationship to processes of behavioral regulation in learning practices:

Principle #1: Experience (in the form of psychological processes) is mediated through artifacts.

Psychological processes such as thinking, feeling, and being (social identity/self) are all mediated by artifacts. Cultural artifacts are both material (e.g., books, computers, pictures, vocal sounds) and symbolic (e.g., sign systems, strategies, social categories, meanings, a community's moral ethos or semiotic sign systems of rights, responsibilities, and obligations). These mediators are cultural resources that make it possible for humans to control and direct behaviors from the outside with others (intermentally) through self-, other-, and co-regulation, all of which are also used in socially shared regulatory processes of group learning. These intermental regulatory processes are appropriated and transformed to control and direct psychological behavior from the inside (intramentally) through self-regulation.

Interestingly, Vygotsky (1929) referred to mediated action as the *cultural habit* of regulating behaviors with others and self to become competent for engaging intellectually, emotionally, and morally in a community's cultural practices. This cultural habit represents a cultural repertoire of valued ways of regulating behavior to develop higher mental functions, that is, those psychological processes controlled with cultural resources – for example, strategies for deliberately focusing attention or strategies for utilizing conceptual tools to enhance or change perception or solve problems. Here, higher mental functions emerge from a fundamentally relational process of mediation, through which individuals control and direct actions, thoughts, and feelings to accomplish goal-directed activities with others. Because self-regulation develops from relational processes of regulatory behaviors with others, it is best thought of as an entangled hybrid of the social and the individual. Thus, self-regulation is not simply about the competencies of an autonomous individual; rather, self-regulation represents an individual's competency for integrating the social with the creative, agential, and authored self to engage in the world in qualitatively new ways – an impressive feat!

Principle #2: The unit of analysis for studying learning and development is "activity."

The "activity" unit of analysis has been elaborated by CHAT scholars as "artifact mediated action" (Cole, 1996), "mediated action" (Wertsch,

1998), "collaborative projects" (Blunden, 2010), and "participation" (Rogoff, 1990). Here, we offer an additional ecological unit of analysis referred to as the "relational habitus" or RH (Stone et al., 2012) to better understand the interrelationship of situated social activity and the emergent micro processes of intersubjectivity (or meaning-making) accomplished through agential actions. In this book, *activity* refers to engagement in historically accumulated forms of cultural practices, including new forms of practices as they emerge and/or develop.

Cultural practices are specifically defined as "a recurrent sequence of goal-directed social activities" that "come packaged with values about what is natural, mature, morally right, or aesthetically pleasing" (Miller & Goodnow, 1995, p. 6; see also Cole, 1995; Scribner & Cole, 1981). A cultural practice (e.g., grooming, cooking, or literacy learning) tends to endure over long periods of time, even though it is made up of short(er)-term activities. Accordingly, *activities* are those types of goal-directed undertakings that create and ultimately modify a practice. For example, science as a cultural practice is made up of goal-directed activities such as planning and conducting investigations, analyzing and interpreting data, and generating and constructing theoretical explanations. Activities like these (and others) come into existence through a range of related "events" that are created through the intersubjective (meaning-making) participation of active agents. These events do not preexist; rather, they are created and negotiated by agents who respond spontaneously and creatively to the uncertainties and ambiguities inherent in sense-making, as well as to their emerging understandings of this process. Through sense-making or intersubjective events with others (co-present or not), agents create their social and cultural world as they utilize mediational artifacts to construct new understandings and knowledge. This process also influences the way in which individuals decide when and how to regulate their cognitive, social-emotional, and volitional behaviors to participate in current and, perhaps, future events. A diagram of the dynamic, unfolding processes of engaging in the events that create activities of a practice is given in Figure 1.1.

A cultural practice is always embedded in a local community, with its historically developed values, moral ethos, and normative expectations about how to regulate behavior for thinking, feeling, doing, and being to accomplish routine activities. Although learners tend to actively instantiate their community's expected and normative ways of regulating behavior, their engagement also brings the potential for changing the community, its practices, and ways of engaging in these practices through behavioral regulation. The potential for transforming a practice emerges from the

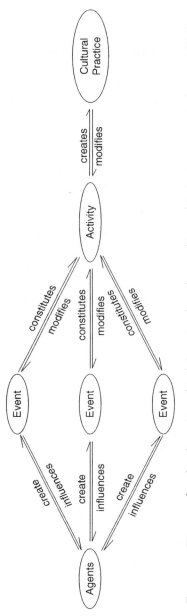

Figure 1.1   Diagram of a cultural practice and its (re)creation through agents' intersubjective engagement in the events (E) that constitute activities (A)

back-and-forth communicative processes of meaning-making, which are always characterized by some degree of "vagueness, ambiguity, and incompleteness" (Rommetveit, 1984, p. 335). These very same characteristics also make it possible to respond to emerging situations (events) with flexibility, creativity, and improvisation. Of course, social interaction is not completely freewheeling, as activities are always influenced by the enabling and constraining influences of a social context.

Utilizing a "practice" lens to understand behavioral regulation in a social setting allows for both conceptualizing and observing how a community's social and cultural history and its resources (norms, values, expectations, ethos, emerging social categories) shape the social organization of agential activities. Activities are agential in the sense that they bring into existence a local field of affordances and constraints that solicit and direct the use of particular forms of behavioral regulation in routine activities (see Dings, 2018). Specifically, contextual affordances are those aspects of a social situation that invite ways of enacting behavioral regulation while contextual constraints direct actions toward some affordances and away from others (Gibson, 1969, 1986). For example, the emergence of practical-moral knowledge (PMK) in learning settings functions as an implicit contextual affordance by directing learners to attend to and use those strategies or material tools (e.g., a journal or notebook) viewed as desirable, preferred, and good. At the same time, PMK tends to constrain attention and usage away from strategies and tools not valued or desired. In effect, a practice lens makes it possible to observe how differing directive aspects of a social context function as a relational resource by contributing to an agent's repertoire of actions and interactions for sense-making, feeling, and thinking with social others. This repertoire of behavior becomes part of how regulatory processes unfold in the present and over time. Of significance, agential learners use their repertoires of behavior creatively, spontaneously, and habitually to transform meaning-making processes as they appropriate and master valued and productive mediational systems for engagement in thinking, feeling, and doing.

Principle #3: Human life is culturally organized through mediational processes and the activities of practices.

Culture becomes a part of human experience/subjectivities (thought, emotions, desires, and volition) primarily through the use of tools and sign systems (language, mathematics, social categories, meanings, diagrams, etc.), but also through time as well as spatial and architectural arrangements in social institutions, all of which mediate activity. This is accomplished by agential individuals who use and transform material and ideational artifacts, such that artifacts develop along with humans. For example, in some informal educational settings, learners begin to construct knowledge about how to interpret and follow directions, enjoy (or dislike) this process, and develop inclinations (or not) to continue. Once competencies develop, it is possible for these very same learners to draw from their experiences to create new activities (as mediational artifacts and tasks) for others to engage in. These examples involve regulating such behaviors as attention, memory, or problem-solving with others through the use of language (sign system) and tools (directions, pictures). Activities like these emerge through a dynamic, ever-changing, relational process of managing uncertainty and ambiguity to make sense of what to do and how to do it with others. In this process, prior ways of regulating behavior may continue or new ways may emerge and be developed, adopted, and/or abandoned over time.

Principle #4: There is a primacy of the social in learning and development.

Children begin the development of their psychological processes as infants, always in relation with social others and always within the social context of cultural practices. In these practices, agents (mothers, fathers, peers) utilize their cultural toolkits (language, strategies, etc.), even if emerging, as a means of regulating their behaviors to assist themselves and others in constructing meanings or understandings. For example, early in life, infants with social others begin to develop competencies with symbol use – even without understanding this competency – when they use pointing gestures to control and direct the attention of their caregivers. As they come to understand how to use concrete and symbolic artifacts through intersubjectivity (meaning-making) with communicative partners (Tomasello, 2000), young children appropriate and potentially change valued forms of psychological life by directing and controlling their actions, interactions, and psychological processes. Thus, the primacy of the social is also an inherent part of mediational processes from which competencies with behavioral regulation emerge during learning activity.

Principle #5: Vygotsky (1978) focused on a genetic (developmental) analysis because he was interested in studying the origins of current psychological phenomena by examining their history.

Vygotsky studied development as emerging outcomes of phylogenetic (evolutionary), cultural-historical, and microgenetic history, with "emerging" signifying that he studied these developmental processes both in real time and over time. Valsiner (2001) aptly calls this approach a "present-to-future model of development ... [that] focuses on the processes of emergence – or construction – of novelty" (p. 86). Valsiner further explains that this semiotic/historical account of development makes it possible "to chart out developmental events *before* these happen" as "anticipated possibilities" (p. 86). One way of "seeing" anticipated possibilities is to focus on how learners regulate their behaviors in real time to engage in learning activities. Real-time activities are *proleptic* or future-oriented, in that they shape future competencies. In other words, what learners can do with assistance over short and long periods of time during learning activities can become their developmental outcomes.

The CHAT approach originates in Vygotsky's grand theory of human learning and development; and, because of his untimely death at the age of thirty-seven, the meanings and implications of his theory continue to be interpreted, refined, and elaborated. The complexity of the theoretical foundations of CHAT make it possible for researchers to use a multidisciplinary approach, drawing from such scholars as Bakhtin (1986), Bourdieu (1977, 1980), Dewey (1938), Duranti and Goodwin (1992), Hutchins (1991), Mead (1934/1962), Ochs (1993, 1996), Peirce (1934), and others to generate new theoretical refinements as closely related lenses for better understanding transactions between the lived world and individuals (see Daniels, 2015). This book contributes to ongoing refinements by offering a combination of analytical concepts – RH, PMK, contextual mood, and identities of competency – for better understanding how learners and the socio-historical contexts of their learning serve to influence and structure engagement in behavioral regulation as a dynamic, emergent, relational, and, at times, a habitual social accomplishment.

We next turn to describing the relationship of the central concepts of a Vygotskian approach to regulatory processes. To do this, we detail how CHAT, as an overarching sociocultural framework, offers the *mediational triangle* as a unique diagram of the activities that create cultural practices. This model offers a useful way of understanding how a community's social and cultural history and its resources contribute to the social organization of agential activity, and how this activity influences and is influenced by active agents as they regulate their cognitive, affective, and volitional behaviors.

Regulatory Processes in Cultural-Historical Psychological Theory

Vygotsky (1966) offers a profoundly original view about behavioral regulation as part of a process of semiotic mediation, the relational mechanism through which culture becomes an inextricable part of our subjectivities (thoughts, ideas, emotions, and motivations). This mediational process, always accomplished with present or nonpresent others, makes possible the development of self-regulated or voluntary control of "elementary" psychological functions such as attention, memory, perception, volition, and emotion (Vygotsky, 1978; Wertsch, 1985a, 1985b). As mentioned in the previous section, artifacts refer to both material tools (pens, written text, words, etc.) and psychological symbols (language or mathematic systems, ideas, concepts, or strategies). By Vygotsky's account, complex higher-order thinking develops from elementary (unmediated) psychological functions when individuals utilize cultural artifacts, and language in particular, to mediate or control and direct these functions. This mediational process enables novices and learners to develop higher-order thinking by controlling and directing their thinking, feelings, and actions as they engage in meaning-making with others. Most importantly, Vygotsky argues that intersubjective processes are at the heart of meaning-making, and these processes actually bring about human learning and development. Intersubjectivity acts as the catalyst of development because humans have the capacity for the semiotic regulation of social, psychological, and volitional behaviors, primarily through spoken language but also through other nonverbal communicative resources such as gestures, tone of voice, or facial expressions. Put simply, individuals as agents use communicative resources to learn how to control and change (regulate) their intellectual, emotional/volitional, and practical competencies. Thus, to understand regulatory processes from a CHAT perspective, it is important to develop ways of seeing how regulatory processes are influenced and shaped by the intersubjective processes of meaning-making, including the utilization of cultural tools and sign systems.

CHAT and the Emergence of Regulatory Processes in Activity

The complexity of a sociocultural approach to regulatory processes as a system in learning practices is made clearer through a cultural-mediational model of activity. The simple model of a mediational triangle shown in Figure 1.2, which is based on Vygotsky's work, is commonly found in early descriptions of CHAT and referred to as the first generation of activity theory (Engeström, 1999). Note that while depictions of CHAT diagrams commonly refer to the participant in activity as the "subject," we use "agent" instead. Following Knappett (2005), we find that "agent" better captures the subject as an "ecological individual" relationally

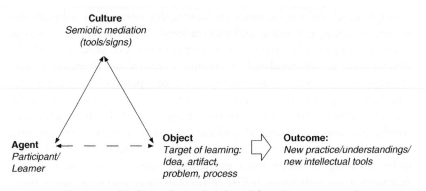

Figure 1.2   Mediational triangle (adapted from Engeström, 1999)

situated in a cultural context; a "psychological agent" who is capable of regulating control over psychological, social, interactional, and practical behaviors; and a "social person" who regulates behavior to inhabit roles as statues associated with culturally valued social identities such as teacher, mentor, parent, or learner (p. 11).

The depiction of mediation in Figure 1.2 illustrates the indirect relationship between an agent in joint activity and their actions on the world (the object), hence the broken line between the agent and the object. A participant's actions on an object are always indirect because they are mediated (changed/reorganized) by cultural artifacts (tools and signs), especially language, which is used by agents to regulate inter- and intrapsychological behaviors during activities. Here, *object* refers to "something" in a learning activity that is perceived or noticed but not yet understood. In this book, *presented problems* often refer to the object of activity. The object, or presented problem, is turned into a meaningful outcome over time through intersubjective processes of meaning-making.

In educational arenas, the "object" typically refers to something that children or novices are learning about and something that the instructor or mentor is trying to teach. For example, in elementary schools where literacy is taught as a joint meaning-making practice, it is common for teachers or mentors to assist learners in how to negotiate the meaning of presented problems, concepts, or ideas with others. Here, problems, concepts, or ideas in the learning activity would be the object, which is perceivable by the senses but not yet (fully) understood. The object is acted on through intersubjective processes to negotiate its meaning with others, which we refer to as problem articulation (see Stone & Gutierrez,

2007). Of course, these very same processes bring into existence the learning activity and, simultaneously, the social context.

According to this early model, the outcomes from meaning-making processes implicitly occur across multiple events in which learners simultaneously construct new knowledge and develop new ways to regulate behavior using mediational means. These new regulatory processes are, in reality, the construction of new mediational devices, that is, new symbolic and material psychological tools (e.g., strategies, plans, texts) for directing and controlling attention, memory, perception, and the like. Competencies with new mediational means create new activities along with new capabilities for regulating behavior in the future. This mediational triangle highlights how meaning-making through semiotic mediation effectively shapes how regulatory processes are enacted as learners develop new ways to regulate their thinking, doing, and being with others. Thus, as Vygotsky (1978) insists, to understand the self-regulation of thought and affect, it is necessary to understand the processes from which they emerge.

Although the basic mediational triangle captures important aspects of an individual acting on the world with mediational means, it does not highlight *time* and *community*. Because of this limitation, representations of this mediational diagram have been further developed by CHAT researchers and scholars. For example, Michael Cole's (1996) treatment of learning and development brings into relief *time* as a fundamental part of the process. Cole clarifies his argument by citing Vygotsky's (1978) "general genetic law of cultural development" in which "functions that initially appear on the interpsychological plane shared between people can then become intrapsychological functions of the individual" over time (as cited in Cole, 1996, p. 274). Vygotsky's explanation of the interrelationship of the individual to the social points to why competency with regulatory processes always begins with social others in routine activities and results in competencies for engaging in a social practice. With the inclusion of time, Cole's (1996) argument also highlights how the processes that create social practices act as a cultural selection mechanism for developmental outcomes over time by utilizing "preexisting mediational systems" as resources for engagement in current activities (p. 275). That is, as learners come to develop competencies for regulating their behaviors with these preexisting mediational means in the present, they are developing new ways and, ultimately, new mediational means to regulate their behavior in future activities.

The inclusion of "time" is captured in Figure 1.3, a representation of a first-generation mediational triangle, which shows t_0 as the initiation of

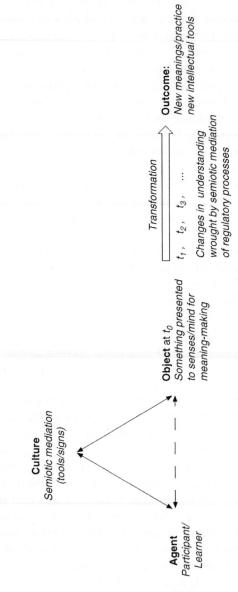

Figure 1.3 An adaptation of a first-generation model of a mediational system showing how the transformation process of an object into meaningful understandings occurs over time. This is successively represented over time by t_0, t_1, t_2, t_3, and so on

the mediational process when the object (a presented problem, an idea, a process, a material item, etc.) is first perceived by a learner/agent. Each of the indicators of the passage of time (t_1, t_2, t_3, etc.) refers to engagement in different instructional or pragmatic events, where knowledge construction is fostered through the semiotic mediation of regulatory processes such as learning to deliberately control attention, memory, or feelings. And, on Vygotsky's account, this mediational process is animated by language as a semiotic resource for making meaning with others.

The process of making meaning out of the "object" contributes to the social formation of our practices, our selves, and our world. Yet this process is neither straightforward nor neutrally benign. Rather, it is a dynamic, situated, opportunistic, and creative process permeated with conflicts and contradictions. The search for meaning with social others is also a complex process, rife with ambiguities and uncertainties and never predetermined. Because of this, the ways in which we regulate our behaviors are always changing, and necessarily involve a shifting mixture of self-, other-, and co-regulation. Cole's (1996) explanation of mediational systems reminds us that, to understand how self-regulation as a competency emerges from engagement in an activity, we must account for "time." Furthermore, time itself is varied, suffused with both turbulence and calm, punctuated by moments of intense activity and quiet reflection, and ripe with potential for creative energy as well as idleness. Across all types of moments, mediational systems of activity can result in dynamic and spontaneous shifts in regulatory processes.

In extant research, the inclusion of time in the mediational processes of learning is generally limited to small periods of time such as a collective lesson or dyadic interactions. Yet time is crucial to understanding Vygotsky's cultural-historical approach (and CHAT in general) as developmental theory rather than simply social learning theory. The import of this will become clearer later in this chapter when we clarify the meaning of Vygotsky's (1978) "zone of proximal development" in relation to systems of mediation found in cultural practices. For now, suffice to say that while the inclusion of time is crucial, first-generation activity theory did not make clear how developmental processes are situated historically, culturally, and socially in communities. Yet Vygotsky (1987) argued that the development of cognitive and social-emotional competencies must be understood in relation to a community and its history of cultural practices. To address this lacuna, Yrjö Engeström (1999, 2008) included other components of an activity system, namely a community level with rules, expectations, values, morals, and a division of labor for who does what, when, and how. Although a theoretical unpackaging of each of these components is not included, they do point to important aspects of cultural practices that influence learning and development in social contexts. For example, the division of labor suggests it is important to examine how the social organization of meaning-making is accomplished in everyday activities. An adaptation of Engeström's model is shown in Figure 1.4 and is referred to as a second-generation model of activity theory.

Engeström's model of a mediational system expands what the transformation of the object entails. In doing so, it emphasizes Vygotsky's fundamental tenet that development needs to be studied not simply as outcomes but as a process, and a relational one at that. For example, the transformation of an object into an outcome is not simply about an individual acting alone but rather about multiple individuals acting together in a semiotic process of meaning-making, hence multiple arrows used to indicate the collaborative transformation of the object into a meaningful outcome. This expansion also highlights an important concept in Vygotsky's (1978) theory, one that is often misunderstood or misinterpreted: the zone of proximal development (ZPD) and its role in learning and developmental processes. Vygotsky defines the ZPD as:

> the distance between the actual developmental level as determined by independent problem solving and the level of potential development as determined through problem solving under adult guidance, or in collaboration with more capable peers. The zone of proximal development defines those functions that have not yet matured but are in the process of maturation, functions that will mature tomorrow but are currently in an embryonic state. These functions could be termed the "buds" or "flowers" of development rather than the "fruits" of development ... what is in the zone of proximal development today will be the actual developmental level tomorrow. (Vygotsky, 1978, pp. 86–87)

Taken out of context, this definition of the ZPD has led to widespread misinterpretations of Vygotsky's ecological approach, namely that instructional assistance is at the heart of this theory. Griffin and Cole (1984) point out that the ZPD is not simply about giving more or less assistance nor about any single assistance strategy in particular learning events. Rather, they argue that the ZPD is about engagement in a "leading activity," that is, an activity that is beyond the learner's current level of competency (Griffin & Cole, 1984, p. 49). The implication is that learning occurs over an aggregate of multiple instructional or learning events through a complex system of mediation. For example, at the beginning of an academic year, first graders might begin their development of story writing by talking over

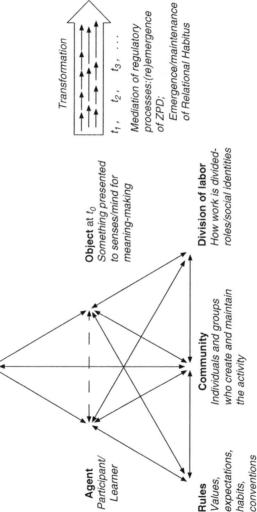

Culture
Semiotic mediation
*System of signs, physical objects
(language, moral ethos, computers)
as resources for regulating
behavior to accomplish activity*

Object at t_0
*Something presented
to senses/mind for
meaning-making*

Agent
*Participant/
Learner*

Rules
*Values,
expectations,
habits,
conventions*

Community
*Individuals and groups
who create and maintain
the activity*

Division of labor
*How work is divided-
roles/social identities*

Transformation

$t_1, \ t_2, \ t_3, \ \ldots$

*Mediation of regulatory
processes:((re)emergence
of ZPD;
Emergence/maintenance
of Relational Habitus*

Outcome:
*New meanings/practice-
new intellectual tools
for regulating behavior*

Community's social and cultural history as resource

Figure 1.4   An adaptation of Engeström's (2008) complex model of mediation in activity

topics of interest in a collective activity (instantiated through a combination of self-, other-, and co-regulation). Then, later on, they might collaboratively or individually regulate their behaviors to draw a picture and associate the picture with a vocabulary word. By the end of the academic year, this activity might involve the same practical procedures or regulatory processes but result in the creation of an elaborate picture with written phrases or sentences. In other words, the children were engaged in learning different aspects of a literacy activity over time through engagement in a range of instructional events. Here, competency for regulating their behavior would develop over time from qualitatively different kinds of assistance, practiced habits, contextual influences (such as rules for engaging), a community's moral ethos and values for using particular social actions, and varying ways of dividing work between learners and their mentors/teachers.

Peter Smagorinsky (2018), in an in-depth analysis of research studies utilizing a Vygotskian approach, has expressed similar views to those of Griffin and Cole (1984). He argues that current treatments of the ZPD do not take into account Vygotsky's central concern with "long-term, socially-mediated human development" (p. 72). Smagorinsky concluded that Vygotsky's (1978) use of growth metaphors, "today" and "tomorrow," has been misinterpreted as only involving short periods of time. As a consequence, and particularly in educational research, the ZPD has been "trivialized" and conflated with the instructional strategy of "scaffold-ing," a conceptual gloss created by Wood, Bruner and Ross (1976). In fact, Smagorinsky's (2018) redefinition of the ZPD as "the zone of next devel-opment" (p. 73) captures a more accurate description of its role in learning and development as a historical (i.e., temporal) process. In this recharac-terization, learners engage in an interrelated cluster of instructional activ-ities over long and short periods of time to develop competencies with the behavioral regulation of psychological and practical processes. That is, the ZPD is not simply about short-term time scales of instructional events in which learners figure out how to solve specific problems. Rather, it is about the combination of short and long periods in which learners begin to utilize mediational systems in learning practices and, over time, develop mastery with regulatory processes to engage more competently in a practice.

Both Griffin and Cole's (1984) and Smagorinsky's (2018) arguments point to why engagement in learning practices results in ZPDs emerging and reemerging over time. This temporal interpretation is a more accurate way of conceptualizing the ZPD and how regulatory processes emerge and change across a combination of synchronic and diachronic timescales. The

ZPD is not a particular kind of assistance in a single learning event; rather, it is developmental phenomena that emerge over time and are mediated by regulatory processes, which themselves are shaped by a broad range of cultural resources. Thus, Cole (1996) refers to mediation in practices as a *system of mediation* that a learner appropriates (takes up and potentially transforms) to engage in behavioral regulation during learning activities.

This system of mediation, by Vygotsky's (1993) own account, represents learners' "interaction with the environment [which] stands at the beginning and at the end" of their development (p. 158). Put differently, agentive learners, utilizing the assistance of others, start with "old" mediational means for regulating behaviors but create new ones as they go along. From this view, the ZPD is embedded in social life and must be viewed as an "interconnected, dynamic, unified whole" with all of its contextual social, moral, and relational influences. For this reason, the social interactional (intersubjective) processes that foster qualitative transformations in elementary psychological functions into higher-order thinking are not simply a matter of scaffolding competent engagement over interactional time. Rather, learners draw from the resources available in a continually emerging context to use and create cultural mediators (psychological signs and material tools) to regulate memory, attention, perception, feelings, reasoning, and problem-solving behaviors in routine activities. In doing so, ways of thinking, feeling, and being become culturally organized through the agential actions of learners in collaboration with the agential actions of social others.

Although the CHAT model of mediation offers very productive ways of observing and documenting changes in practices over time, few studies have examined the social organization of intersubjectivity, which is the meaning-making activity so fundamental to fostering learning and development. The reason for this, in our view, is related to an emphasis on the guiding elements of an activity (e.g., artifacts, rules, division of labor) in the mediational diagram of activity (see Figure 1.1) rather than an emphasis on the fundamental role of intersubjective processes in bringing about the social formation of mind and self. To contribute to the CHAT approach, we have developed a relatively new relational unit of analysis: the relational habitus (RH), explained in greater depth in Chapter 2 (see also Stone et al., 2012). Goodnow and Lawrence (2015) suggest that the RH offers "an innovative and more integrative" way of accounting for how a social context as well as active learners influence the relational, material, and spatial organization of intersubjectivity as the meaning-making process that stimulates learning and development. As an analytical unit, the RH does not simply focus on the social interactions that give rise to meaning-making; instead, it brings into relief significant influences of the social, material, spatial, and historical context on the social construction of selves, knowledge, and culture through intersubjectivity. For this reason, the RH is both a relational unit of analysis and a way to observe how intersubjectivity as a mediational, contextual, and relational process impacts how learners regulate their behaviors to use mediational means and construct new meanings and understandings of the "object" of activity as well as new feelings about it.

Of import, the RH as an ensemble of selves, tools, tasks, and others makes visible the interactive aspects of regulatory processes open to observation. These processes are cognitive, emotional, volitional, moral, and agential in the Vygotskian sense of coming into play in a sociocultural context, rather than in the sense of being an individual process or individually internalized. They can be "seen" in practice when we examine three types of regulatory processes that are influenced by the social context and take place in learning activities – other-regulation, co-regulation, and self-regulation, all of which are components of socially shared regulation occurring in group-learning activities. The definitions that follow for each of three basic forms of behavioral regulation were derived utilizing a social practice lens.

In learning activities, *other-regulation* encompasses social acts of instruction or guidance that involve obligatory directives or orienting requests for implementing an action in a prescribed manner, to maintain or enact goal-directed activity. Other-regulation is enacted by teachers, mentors or caregivers, and/or peers to prompt others to initiate and carry out the pragmatic actions of an activity. Engagement in other-regulation involves an agentive, intentional action by one person on another that may require regulating practice, cognition, affect, or volition. This definition, however, does not necessarily mean that the "other" is passive or nonagentive. On the contrary, the other can be called on to act creatively and agentively, either as a potentially knowledgeable peer or as a less-knowledgeable novice. In the RH, neither the self nor the other are isolated entities but rather key actors among others. Together, the self and the other are optimally collaborators or co-conspirators in the culturally figured world of the learning activity. This is the case whether their interactions are strictly hierarchical or relatively egalitarian. But, in other-regulation, the one directing the other takes the dominant role in the activity.

In contrast, *co-regulation* involves collaborative social acts in which learners (and teachers, mentors, parents, or peers) take into account another's perspective on a problem or task to negotiate and co-construct understanding, knowledge, and/or feelings. This form of regulation includes the collaborative use of tools and texts to coordinate and maintain goal-directed learning activities. In this regulatory process, the conscious construction or co-construction of tools, texts, and tasks in framing the activity is paramount to how the sociocultural system of activity is established. Even more so than with other-regulation, the self and the other(s) in co-regulation are mutually implicated both in the act of configuring the system of activity and in carrying out the tasks and activities that are integral to that sociocultural system.

Finally, *self-regulation* involves a person's own cognitive, social, emotional, and volitional actions in the pursuit of understanding through the use of tools and texts in implementing and maintaining goal-directed activity. Although initiated autonomously, the self's actions are nonetheless enacted within a culturally figured world of shared understandings and meanings. These meanings are shaped by a community's rules, norms, expectations, values, and moral ethos, that is, a continually emerging local semiotic (sign) system of rights, responsibilities, and duties that establishes legitimate ways of controlling and directing actions and interactions for competent participation. These aspects of a culturally figured world have been developmentally established and implicitly appropriated in successive habitual and/or improvisational acts of participation in the activity as framed by the social organization of the RH. The self in self-regulation is an active navigator in a sociocultural terrain in which one's knowledge and skills in relation to the tools and tasks at hand are called into play. Typically, the motivation is to situate the self as a responsive and responsible actor in a leading activity, making the self not only a participant but also an anticipator of the navigational field of activity and thus, finally, an authoritative initiator of the activity – that is, the author of one's own learning.

The RH as a relationship to tools, task, and others characterizes the enactment of all forms of regulatory processes. The relational characteristic of these processes is always influenced explicitly and implicitly by agential learners and their social and historical context. The RH highlights how these influences act together over interactional time. What is more, it provides a way of documenting how each element of the RH is involved in the social organization of meaning-making (intersubjectivity) through behavioral regulation. Understanding these influences can reveal how the social context both affords and constrains agential acts involving novel, spontaneous, and opportunistic as well as habitual and recurrent ways of regulating behavior. Observing regulatory process through the RH makes it possible to understand how learning occurs through different aspects of the developmental process, whether through changes in participation, in understandings, or in creating interpretive frames, social identities, volitional inclinations, moral knowledge, or the social context. Through all of these aspects of learning and development, learners utilize intersubjective processes, socially organized by the RH, to transform the object of an activity into a meaningful outcome through regulatory processes, resulting in cognitive, affective, and volitional competencies and/or new understandings about academic content or everyday life.

CHAPTER 2

The Relational Habitus and Regulatory Processes

Learning arenas, formal and informal, emerge from everyday life. Out of the fabric of our social contexts and all their complex interweavings of experiences and communicative practices, individuals (learn to) regulate their own and others' ways of being, thinking, and feeling. The forms of behavioral regulation that occur during the routine social practices of learning, play, and work have the potential to qualitatively transform intellectual and social lives. Learners' entanglements in eventful and meaningful arenas of activity – whether living spaces, classrooms, after-school clubs, or home environments – are spaces where a repertoire of cultural resources (sign systems and tools) can be utilized to construct shared understandings in relation to given and emergent problems or tasks. The constellation of self, tools, and tasks in relation to others in the social scene represents an ecological ensemble that we refer to as the *relational habitus* (RH). Through the RH, the combined processes of self-, other-, and co-regulation are structured and emerge through engagement in the actions and interactions that simultaneously create learning contexts, frame learning activities, and foster cognitive, emotional, and social competencies. In effect, the RH is a conceptual and practical tool for understanding the reciprocal relationship between a learner's engagement in regulatory processes and the socio-historical, temporal, and spatial environments in which that engagement takes place.

Whether as a tool for observing regulatory processes in social contexts or as a unit of analysis for research, the RH is defined as an ecological ensemble of relations including self, tools, tasks, and others that is intersubjectively constructed and sustained over time in formal and informal learning communities. Here, *ecological* refers to the natural, social, and built environments of humans while *intersubjective* signifies the social and psychological processes of communicative meaning-making. Intersubjectivity fosters learning and development and therefore undergirds all regulatory processes (Stone et al., 2012; Vygotsky, 1978). Understanding what an RH is and how it functions allows us to approach learning not as a mysterious event inside an individual's mind but as an observable interactional event. Furthermore, the RH permits us to observe how learners control and direct their behavior during joint activity, which affects how learning unfolds. In this way, the RH is an effective tool for reflecting on and potentially changing the social organization of intersubjective processes that influence and even transform learning engagement, both present and future.

This chapter will explain recent conceptualizations of intersubjectivity and their connections to the RH. We will explain the value of RH as a conceptual and pragmatic tool for understanding the relationship between learners' engagement in regulatory processes and the social construction of learning contexts. We will also describe each relational aspect of the RH as an intertwined and interconnected part of regulatory processes. Finally, we will present examples of the RH taken from video ethnographies of formal and informal learning settings.

Intersubjectivity: Beyond Consensus

Intersubjectivity is commonly defined as a consensual process in which face-to-face negotiations of thoughts and ideas produce a mutual understanding or shared meaning between learners and teachers, novices and experts, and/or peers (Edwards & Mercer, 1987; Göncü, 1993; Kozulin, 1990). In this process, children and adults exploit semiotic resources and sign systems that are both linguistic (word choice, grammar, etc.) and paralinguistic (volume, intonation, gestures, etc.) to build new understandings over interactional time. As learners engage in the semiotic meaning-making processes of intersubjectivity, they are presumed to be simultaneously engaging in behavioral regulation, whether co-, self-, or other-regulation, or some combination of these. A weakness of this consensual process view of intersubjectivity is that it does not adequately account for how learning contexts influence intersubjectivity, nor does it address how this influence structures engagement in regulatory processes over time. In fact, a consistent focus on the cognitive processes of negotiating shared understandings during dyadic and/or face-to-face interactions has prevented a more nuanced view of context from catching hold. When researchers focus on dyadic interactions (whether learner–learner or teacher/mentor–learners), then social and material contexts and their influence on regulatory processes are simply left out. This limitation has led to a growing sea change in perspectives on intersubjectivity and therefore on regulatory processes.

In the past couple of decades, researchers have uncovered a range of complexities that demonstrate why the consensual/cognitive view is inadequate for describing intersubjective processes in learning settings. A more elaborated definition is emerging that points to how intersubjectivity necessarily involves a condition of *cultural relatedness* that precedes pragmatic, face-to-face processes of regulating behavior and negotiating shared meanings. Cultural relatedness entails a sense of people co-experiencing a mutually shared world when they enter into any context. That is, when individuals come into contact in a cultural setting, they assume that others experience the world in the same way in the same place (Duranti, 2010). This assumption of experiential sharedness implies a pervasive sense of relatedness and this means that intersubjectivity is a *cultural condition of social life* in familiar as well as unfamiliar settings. The pervasive sense of relatedness means that intersubjectivity is a precondition of all communicative processes; simultaneously, it is influenced by prior experiences of regulating meaning-making behavior in particular contexts. Most importantly, as a precondition to communication, intersubjectivity does not imply agreement so much as shared understandings for how to interpret and create a situation. In other words, there is some common foundation from which to negotiate a shared view. This common foundation may be based on implicit or explicit communicative resources, which makes possible intersubjective meaning-making through conflict and contention, agreement and accord, and/or anything in between. Intersubjectivity as a cultural condition of social life means that, when individuals come into cultural contexts like classrooms, after-school clubs, playgrounds, and so on, they bring with them an awareness of others, whether those others are co-present or not. This awareness shapes how they then engage in the communicative processes of intersubjectivity to construct mutual understandings.

The social awareness of others also brings an awareness of how past (historical) intersubjective interactions were accomplished through behavioral regulation. The control and direction of behaviors, however, do not simply involve interactions between individual learners, teachers, or mentors. Rather, such interactions invariably include tasks and/or emergent/ presented problems as well as the use of tools to accomplish them. All of these components of goal-directed activities – selves, tools, tasks, and others – come into play as learners regulate their behaviors to engage in meaning-making. Yet analyses of dyadic talk between learners and teachers, or caregivers and children, which are common to many studies of intersubjectivity, capture neither the complexity of these relational processes nor their interrelatedness with the contextual structuring of behavioral regulation.

Relatedness and the Relational Habitus

Because human intersubjectivity is so implicit and so intricately embedded in how we learn, the process of learning can seem like a mysterious, almost indecipherable phenomenon. The concept of the RH enables us to identify and interpret the observable features of this process. In effect, it provides an analytical tool for observing and reflecting on the complexity of regulatory processes used in the intersubjective processes of meaning-making. This analytical tool opens up the human sense of relatedness, or the social awareness of others, in cultural contexts. Specifically, RH approaches selves, tools, tasks, and others as an ecological ensemble that influences the moment-to-moment processes of intersubjectivity and, by extension, the regulatory processes in learning activities. The RH is therefore both a research and a practical tool for making regulatory processes visible, analyzing them, and evaluating them. For educators, in and out of schools, the RH can be used to act on and structure two aspects of the intersubjective processes of learning: (1) the contextual structuring of intersubjectivity and (2) the emergent processes of intersubjectivity over interactional time. Being able to observe and structure both of these aspects opens up new possibilities for designing instructional strategies to assist learners to make use of the resources at hand, regulate behavior (their own and that of others) in productive ways, and be (more) engaged in knowledge construction.

In goal-directed activities, the routine and repeated actions and interactions that occur within an ensemble of selves, tools, tasks, and others serve to produce a specialized relatedness, a type of relationality that situates an individual as an integral part of a dynamic and ecological system of relationships and interconnections. Each component (selves, tools, tasks, and others) becomes *an automatic part* of embodied regulatory actions and interactions of learning. The interrelationship between the RH, regulated behaviors, and intersubjectivity is shown in Figure 2.1. Recall that the RH highlights the social and relational aspects of intersubjective processes and is therefore influenced by the rules, values, expectations, division of labor, and practical-moral knowledge of a community. (See Figure 1.4 to view how

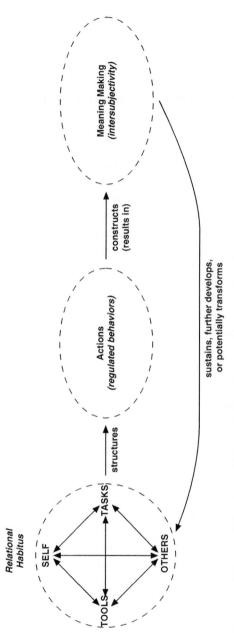

Figure 2.1   Diagram of the relational habitus (RH) and how it influences and is influenced by the regulated actions of meaning-making in social practices

the RH is situated in a complex model of mediation in activity where the object is turned into a meaningful outcome.)

The RH structures regulated actions even as it establishes and maintains the culturally defined range of actions that are possible and/or preferable in the relevant setting. Within a setting, individuals act on the tasks before them with the tools at hand. As they do so, they may or may not remain within the range of locally acceptable or locally preferred actions. At the same time, individuals account for and act on their own developing relations to others within the setting. Through the entangled relatedness of all these aspects, regulatory processes emerge from embodied actions – whether intentional or not – and sociocultural understandings as well as meanings are constructed. When (or if) such task structures become a common occurrence, the relevant communicative procedures, as shaped by regulatory processes, become part of learners' repertoires, potentially influencing the habitual ways they engage in the intersubjective processes of meaning-making. In this way, the RH emerges from and sustains particular relationships among selves, tools, tasks, and others, just as it shapes future regulatory processes. In sum, the RH is an emerging ensemble that – whether sustained, transformed, or challenged – naturally becomes part of and continues to shape regulatory processes. No matter how learning events unfold over time, the RH influences how learners make meaning. To further explicate how the RH emerges, we turn now to a brief description of each of its components.

Relationship with Others

Social *relationships*, according to Vygotsky (1981), underlie the emergence of feelings and complex thinking that is, he argues, accomplished through intersubjectivity. Through coordinated and collaborative action, relationships to others are constructed and sustained over time – that is, people construct their thinking, feelings, and being among others within sociohistorical contexts. Not unexpectedly, there are significant differences created in the development of relationships through the design of learning tasks, whether informally or formally defined. For instance, in a classroom, when young children are instructed to write a story individually and to ask for help when needed, the relationship among learners is influenced by an unspoken orientation that gives priority to individuals and their accomplishments. It makes sense from this orientation that learners will engage in intersubjective processes, that is, self-regulate their behavior, to ask for clarification about directions, responsibilities, and/or tasks. While this type of self-regulation would aim at helping individuals (the *self*) acquire competency, the relationship that emerges between learners is still an interpersonal one (albeit one where the primary emphasis is on how an individual student can take responsibility for gaining competency). This influences how tasks are interpreted in relation to others as well as how tools are used in relation to others. In contrast, in a classroom where learners are instructed to write stories in collaboration with others (i.e., collaborative learning/peer group), different relationships evolve and different behavioral regulation strategies will be accomplished through different intersubjective processes. Here, one might find a collaborative perspective in which learners are oriented to construct knowledge for themselves as well as "make it [their] own in a community" (Bruner, 1996, p. 172). In other words, historically constructed relationships with others within goal-directed activities bring into play expected (and sometimes unexpected) ways of achieving and displaying competency through behavioral regulation.

Because expectations in learning activities are produced through intersubjective processes of communication, the voices and other agential actions of learners (regulatory actions) bring dialogic traces of previous contexts into the (re)negotiation of social relationships in activity (Bakhtin, 1981). The social relationships that emerge and the work that is produced through these relationships, both in the present and in the past, also serve to build the larger cultural landscape of learning arenas over time. This building of a local context contributes to the cultural aspect of intersubjectivity, that is, the condition of relatedness that precedes the face-to-face pragmatic processes of regulating behavior to negotiate shared meanings. Importantly, awareness of others is not deterministic and does not guarantee how intersubjectivity will play out. On the contrary, learners play a significant agential role in their own and each other's regulatory processes of learning. Likewise, they actively participate in the historical development of the local culture (learning context). Consequently, the inclination to regulate behavior and the values attached to that regulation are influenced not only by individual perceptions but also by individuals' engagement in a history of relational and meaning-making processes, as well as how that engagement is evaluated and marked as valuable (or not) within the cultural context. Because the production of value is part of a bidirectional relationship, all roles used to inhabit social identities within a learning environment (child, adult, learner, teacher, student, peer, helper, etc.) can and do play defining parts in how the relational habitus is organized for engagement in behavioral regulation and how this leads to the development of psychological competencies.

Relationship to Tools

In almost any human activity, relationships with others are intricately connected to tools. Recently, individual relationships to tools and their mediating role in learning have become an important research focus (Holland & Cole, 1995; Janlert & Stolterman, 1997; Knappett & Malafouris, 2008). The reason for this attention is related to the growing understanding that the meaning of tools always "originate(s) . . . in the world of social relations" (Kozulin, 1986, p. 62). Vygotsky (1978) prefigured this focus and rendered it most clearly with his statement, "The path from object to child and from child to object passes through another person" (p. 30). Mirroring similar sentiments, Blumer (1969) claims that "the meaning of a thing (tool) for a person grows out of the ways in which other persons act toward the person with regard to the thing" (p. 4). According to Cole (1996), tools and their mediational properties have "developmental histories'" arising from their use in prior activities and their use in the regulatory processes of present learning activities. The key point here is that it is impossible to understand the meaning of a tool during regulatory processes without seeing it as an inherent part of the selves, tools, tasks, and others ensemble. Tools (whether language, books, computers, paper, pencil, etc.) take on meaning in the context of their relationship with others and this relationship becomes an essential aspect of how learners regulate their behaviors to accomplish tasks. Through repeated interactions with tools, children develop understandings and expectations about how to construct meaning, both independently and in collaboration with others. As they do so, they make inferences about how best to utilize tools to regulate their own and others' behavior through the intersubjective processes of knowledge construction. Further, the meaning of tools continually develops as learners and teachers/mentors build new understandings of their relationships to tasks and others. Past use of tools (whether independently or in cooperation with others) influences the social organization of present and future actions, thereby shaping how individuals regulate their behaviors in the meaning-making processes of learning. Because of this, tools and their meanings are not static but develop and change over time. Ultimately, understanding the relational aspects of tools allows educators and researchers to examine the dynamics by which novices learn to recognize and use them. Even more importantly, it provides us means of observing, analyzing, assessing, and potentially shaping the regulatory processes that take place in learning activities.

Relationship to Tasks

Formally defined, a task is simply a piece of work assigned for completion. In educational research, the definition of a task becomes more specified, indicating a formally assigned problem, referred to by Getzels (1975) as the presented problem. Presented problems are characteristic of classroom learning environments, in which possible solution(s) and processes to achieve these solutions are already known to the teacher but not necessarily to the students. As presented problems, tasks are viewed as a unit of work with pragmatic significance and clearly defined outcomes (Ellis, 2003). In general, presented problems are assumed to refer to a range of activities, from simple and brief exercises to more complex and lengthy activities. A growing body of educational research has shown how the structure of presented problems influences learning (e.g., Chizhik, 2001; Lodewyk et al., 2009). Underlying this work, however, is a psychological paradigm that examines the intramental aspects of how tasks or problems are solved. Within this paradigm, only mental processes and content organization are used to explain behavioral regulation and language. Consequently, the ways in which regulatory processes emerge from learners' developing relationships to tasks, tools, and other people on the scene are absent from this body of work.

From a relational habitus perspective, on the other hand, tasks are not simply units of work that are fully defined by teachers for students. Rather, tasks in the form of presented problems are better conceived of as an essential part of *problem articulation*, which involves both what is stated in the presented problem and the implicit rules, norms, and strategies for how to regulate behavior during problem-solving (Stone, 1996; Stone & Gutierrez, 1999). As such, tasks are the "object" of activity and therefore part of a dynamic, ecological, and relational process of sense-making, that is, intersubjectivity. Although there may be structure in how a problem is presented, or some initial understanding of its solution, the meaning of the task only comes to make sense through intersubjective processes. These sense-making processes are not fully open to agential action (i.e., our ability to affect and control ourselves and our world) but are partially constrained by prior coordinated modes of participation, which inform the local cultural sense of "the world as it presents itself" or the "existential condition that can lead to a shared understanding" (Duranti, 2010, p. 6). This cultural aspect of intersubjectivity necessarily shapes how learners regulate their engagement with tasks. However, because of individual agency within activity, historical constraints on action influence rather than determine the face-to-face interactions through which the meaning of a task arises. For example, a teacher may either impose a specific task on students or merely set the frame for it; in either case, the learners, whether through resistance or cooperation or something in between, can transform the task into something other than what the teacher had originally envisioned. In this sense, managing learning in an educational setting is a study in task negotiation. Through these processes, tasks become part of the relational habitus. Simultaneously, competency becomes co-constructed through the regulatory practices that emerge from the social organization of intersubjectivity.

Relational Habitus: In Formal and Informal Learning Arenas

To illustrate how the contextual structuring of the RH influences the emergence and structure of regulatory processes over interactional time, we will utilize excerpts taken from video ethnographies conducted in one formal and one informal learning setting. Each excerpt will display the social organization of the relational habitus and how it structures intersubjective processes of meaning-making.

Relational Habitus in Mr. Minton's Classroom

The formal learning setting is a sixth-grade classroom where the teacher, Mr. Minton, created a learning culture that marked students' thinking as valuable, desired, and necessary for engagement. To create this culture, he positioned himself as someone who collaborated with students in seeking out solutions and who, at times, would share his own expertise. Mr. Minton also consistently used linguistic resources, such as modal verbs of possibility (could, might, would), to position the students as agents in determining the use of a broad array of available resources, which included strategies, hunches, journal writing, help seeking, and prior experiences, among many others. Minton's presented problems were designed to be generative meaning-making devices that students could use collaboratively and individually to create their own solution methods, construct understandings, and interpret the assigned tasks. As a consequence, the relational habitus that emerged here had the effect of structuring and sustaining communicative processes of intersubjectivity as struggles for meaning. These meaning-making struggles involved students co-regulating their behaviors to accomplish different forms of negotiations, including conflicts and disagreements, help-seeking and help-giving actions, agreements, and, quite often, humor.

Excerpt 2.1 shows how the RH in Mr. Minton's classroom is organized as dynamic shifts between self-, other-, and co-regulation, with an emphasis on co-regulation. The excerpt begins as one of the students, Alise, who is covering her mouth and using private speech, realigns with her small group (Emily, Nerses, and Austin). Alise utilizes previously written notes in her journal in an attempt to understand accented syllables in a line of poetry taken from "The Geese" by Richard Peck, which has been written on the front board: "My father was the first to hear the passing of the geese each year."

As Alise shifts from private speech to face-to-face participation, she makes observable how the RH is configured here to create opportunities for co-regulation with her peers (Nerses and Emily). Alise initiates verbal engagement by saying, "I: do-n't get this:" while glancing around the table to accomplish an implicit help-seeking request with both verbal language and gestures. This is an expected way of initiating co-regulation in Mr. Minton's class. Through this request Alise positions herself as a novice who can actively self-regulate her behavior to control the situation, in this case, to gain an understanding of syllabic stress. Simultaneously, Alise positions her interlocutors as knowledgeable agents with help-giving competencies. This interpersonal positioning gives Alise's peers an opportunity to assist her by using (other) resources at hand. In this way, Alise's peers also engage in the co-regulation of their behaviors to co-construct knowledge.

The ways in which Alise's peers respond illustrate how this local RH structures intersubjective processes that result in fluid moves between self-, other-, and co-regulation. Alise's positioning bid is taken up readily by Nerses and Emily, although in different ways. Nerses acknowledges Alise's indirect request for help by glancing at her and then at Emily (line 2.04). Emily aligns with Alise by agreeing, "ah yeah" and evaluates syllabic stress as "weird." This combination of speech acts displays Emily's agreement that syllabic stress is difficult to understand and also confirms that Alise's implicit request for help is reasonable. This acknowledgement works to soften the immediate obligatory directive (and strategy) proffered by Emily, "you just have to say it like like (.) my ↑fa::ther::" (lines 2.05–2.06). This softening of a directive mirrors Mr. Minton's typical

Excerpt 2.1 *The dynamic pattern of regulation*

Alise:	((*Puts her hand down from her mouth, turns and leans into*	2.01
	the group. Glances quickly around the table.))	2.02
	I: do ↑ n't get this:	2.03
Nerses:	((*Looks up from his writing and looks at Alise and Emily.*))	2.04
Emily:	((*To Alise.*)) ah yeah, it's weird. you just have to say it like	2.05
	like (.) my ↑fa::ther::	2.06
Alise:	((*Looks rapidly between Emily and her notebook while Emily*	2.07
	is talking.))	2.08
Nerses:	((*Looking up and smiling.*))	2.09
Alise:	((*Laughs.*)) my ↑fa::ther::= ((*Sing-song voice, smiling,*	2.10
	moving her body in a rhythmic motion with her talk. Looks	2.11
	towards the front of the class then briefly at her notebook and	2.12
	then back up to Emily.))= [was. the ↑f::irst: to hear °ok°*	2.13
Emily	[the firs:t	2.14
Alise:	what if you didn't say it like that. (hhh.)	2.15
	((*Alise's gaze shifts rapidly between Emily and Austin several*	2.16
	times as she asks this question.))	2.17
Emily	yeah you just have ta[	2.18
Alise:	((*giggling*)) [not everyone goes my [↑fa::ther::	2.19
	[(((*Raises her*	2.20
	eyebrows and shifts her shoulders upward.))	2.21
Emily:	[I know you just have ta. (..)	2.22
Nerses:	[(((*Nerses looks up from this paper toward the group. He*	2.23
	smiles widely and laughs slightly.))	2.24
Alise:	[(((*Alise looks back to her notebook.*))	2.25
Emily:	=you just have ta[=	2.26
Nerses:	[I am your fa::th::er:	2.27
	((*In a low voice-imitating Darth Vader while smiling, then*	2.28
	returns to working in his notebook.))	2.29
Alise:	((*Laughs.*)) ((*Reads a different line from board to group.*))	2.30
	I'll tell you the story of Jimmy Jet and you'll know what I tell	2.31
	you is true. I didn't see >any [accent!<	2.32
	[(((*Accentuates "accent"*	2.33
	with a quick hand gesture.))	2.34
	can somebody help me with this?	2.35
	((*Glances around the group beginning with Nerses and*	2.36
	ending with Austin. She returns gaze to middle of table	2.37
	and waits for a response.))	2.28

methods of attenuating his authority toward evaluating knowledge production. For this reason, Emily's directive is a bid to other-regulate but it is a hedged bid. By hedging, she is both providing a strategy and aligning with Alise as a collaborator in the participant role of help giver. Meanwhile,

Nerses humorously employs a pop culture reference (the voice of the *Star Wars* character Darth Vader) to exaggerate syllabic stress ("I am your fa:: th::er:"), illustrating how a variety of resources was seen as competent and desirable for the co-construction of knowledge in this setting. Altogether, we see the students drawing from their relationship to tools, tasks, and others (i.e., the relational habitus) to interactively collaborate in knowledge construction, using self-, other-, and co-regulation to gain competency and master the tasks at hand.

Next, Alise revoices Emily's strategy for figuring out syllabic stress, "my ↑fa::ther::" (line 2.10). This is an intersubjective uptake of Emily's strategy and evidence of a shift to co-regulation. After reading the line of poetry from the board, Alise asks, "what if you didn't say it like that," as she looks to the members of her small group. Alise's question, which is another initiation of co-regulation, leads Emily to repeatedly offer an imperative; specifically, she directs Alise to pronounce "father" in a particular way (lines 2.18, 2.22, 2.26). The use of imperative grammatical constructions or obligatory directives have been found to close down talk in learning events and call for action over reflection (see Wagner & Herbel-Eisenmann, 2008). However, Emily's directive ("just have ta") does not have this effect. Instead, Alise continues to pursue the problem of figuring out accented syllables, explicitly asking for help ("can somebody help me with this?") as she glances at her group members. In fact, obligatory directives (other-regulation) were not common in Mr. Minton's instructional discourse; instead, he tended to use modal constructions to shift the responsibility for knowledge construction into the hands of the students. As illustrated in Excerpt 2.1, when obligatory directives did not lead to understanding, learners turned to co-regulation in their continued attempts for meaning-making. Alise's ongoing search for understanding was related to how the local cultural context structured the interrelationship of selves, tools, tasks, and others to construct meanings (relational habitus).

In this classroom environment, students interpreted tasks as opportunities for collaborative meaning-making, or co-regulation of learning. This mode of participation, of course, influenced the students' selection of communicative resources, which was itself a form of self-regulation. As noted in our discussion in "Intersubjectivity: Beyond Consensus," however, self-regulation is about more than the individual; specifically, it is about an individual's relationship with tools, tasks, and others. Here, students persistently regulated their behavior to pursue understanding by interacting with others and requesting help even in the face of difficulties – a common pattern in Mr. Minton's classroom.

Taken as a whole, the data from Mr. Minton's classroom illustrate how a learning context emerges. In both whole- and small-group learning, collaboration and negotiation were marked as preferred and desired ways to regulate behavior to construct meaning through intersubjectivity. The relational habitus arose from and reinforced this preference. In effect, the RH structured the relationships between individuals, tools, tasks, and others such that learners automatically and habitually engaged in a dynamically shifting pattern of self-, other-, and co-regulation. This pattern created a form of perspective-taking about engagement that resulted in a community where shared agency and shared responsibility for assessing and constructing knowledge implicitly influenced future regulatory actions. Thus, the RH shapes not only how perspective-taking occurs during the interactional processes of intersubjectivity but also how this process can lead to perspective-making. Over time, the creation of new perspectives can reorganize how behaviors are regulated during meaning-making with others.

So far, we have shown how the emergent and sustained RH in a formal learning setting structured regulatory processes of meaning-making. In the case of Mr. Minton's classroom, meaning-making was structured mostly as collaborative, and co-regulation was especially emphasized as a preferred regulatory process. In Excerpt 2.1, the task, or presented problem, was not ambiguous – learners had to make sense out of a line of poetry. The task is necessarily shaped within the context of the relational habitus that emerged in Mr. Minton's class. Here, the task at hand (making meaning out of a line of poetry) was framed as a joint activity among peers, whose implicit knowledge was respected. While the children's knowledge was sometimes challenged by Mr. Minton, he acted less as an arbiter of action and more as a resource for mobilizing the tools of pragmatic action. Because the students' collective knowledge was honored, there is an implicit under-standing among the students that makes it acceptable for each of them to have only partial knowledge. Put differently, the children do not have to construct meaning alone; instead, they can do it collaboratively. For these reasons, Alise feels comfortable expressing an initial lack of understanding. Emily agrees with Alise in seeing the difficulty but immediately suggests a distinctive sociolinguistic "reading" of the line. The others in the group, recognizing their status as knowledgeable peers, question Alise's "reading" and wonder if there are other possible readings. Alise, referring to the tools at hand (the poetic line on the board in front of them), accepts the others' questions as legitimate and repeats her request for peer assistance. The task, tools, selves, and others involved in this sociocultural activity are all called into play according to the relational habitus that the teacher and the students have historically established in their classroom.

Relational Habitus in a Playful Learning World

The Fifth Dimension (5thD) after-school programs present a unique approach to after-school learning (Cole, 1996, 2003). Drawing from Vygotskian and neo-Vygotskian theories of intellectual and social-emotional development, the 5thD creates informal learning environments that nurture robust academic competencies through a combination of play and project learning. In the 5thD, children engage in activities with the help of an imaginary cyberspace entity referred to as the "Wizard" (also known as the "Wiz"). Other important mentors at 5thD sites are the Wizard Assistants (WAs), all of whom are undergraduates from local universities, where they are enrolled in courses focused on cultural-historical psychological theories of human development.

Here, to further illustrate how the RH structures intersubjectivity accomplished through regulatory processes, we utilize an excerpt taken from a 5thD site located in northern California. At this particular site, known as the Magical Web, or simply, "The Web," the WAs are enrolled in a college course focused on the interrelationship between learning and development. This course emphasized the role of discourse (i.e., what is said and what is done) in creating a proleptic approach to mentoring. Prolepsis involves treating learners as competent in activities that are currently beyond their developmental level. Therefore, these particular undergraduates learned how to interact with children by treating them as competent even when competency was still emerging. This proleptic instructional approach was complemented by open-ended presented pro-blems or tasks. Take, for example, a message sent by the Wiz to the children of The Web (Excerpt 2.2), which ultimately inspired a garden project.

Excerpt 2.2 *Open-ended task sent by the Wiz*

I keep hearing about the northern California "Farm to Fork" and "organic gardening" movements. I am intrigued! The Magical Web is a Fifth Dimension Club in the middle of the green belt of organic gardening where you too could be part of sustainable and responsible organic gardening. What lucky citizens of the 5th D you are! I am convinced the Magical Web could be part of this movement. I have a challenge for you since your community is becoming so famous: Develop your own organic garden and contribute to your community by investigating and creating a garden and by sharing your results. For this challenge, you will need to work with other citizens in the 5th Dimension who want to help you become part of this famous movement. Don't forget to invite a Wizard's Assistant!

Keep me posted!
The Wiz

The Wiz's communication structures the "problem to be solved" as a collaborative one. What is more, it positioned the children as the creators, planners, and implementers of the project. This agential positioning of children as having control over the pragmatic definition of the task and the problem-solving process emerged in part due to the relative ambiguity of the presented problem, which included no explicit procedures for a solution. This open and agential approach to project learning in The Web became a norm for the participating children and their mentors. Over time, the relational habitus in this setting encouraged regulatory processes that were animated by figuring out how and what to do with others in relation to the tasks and tools at hand.

In Excerpt 2.3, Jak (eleven years old), Paige and Sarah (both ten years old), Lulu (eight years old), and Keith (seven years old) are sitting with Becca (a WA) at a small rectangular table. The children are trying to figure out what supplies they need to create their garden. Meanwhile the WA, Becca, is documenting their ideas.

The typical social organization of the RH in the Web is captured in Excerpt 2.3, which shows how the RH structures intersubjective interactions as collaborative negotiations that created a relationship between the children and their task (problem) such that each member of the group had the rights to co-regulate behavior by proposing a plan (strategy) for future actions utilizing tools (in this case, seeds for gardening). This form of RH, built around collaboration, encouraged the children to co-regulate their behaviors to engage in intersubjectivity through polite and sometimes explicit directives for specific solutions as well as justifications for those solutions.

The process of collaborative negotiation (co-regulation) is initiated when Jak suggests a practical strategy, that is, they should begin by getting "seeds." Accordingly, Jak offers a justification indicating that his proposed strategy is a collaborative desire, that is, what the group wants ("what all we want:↑"). Although his suggestion is accomplished with what appears to be a strong directive utilizing the modal verb *should* ("we should"), the inclusion of "I think" functions as a hedge. This hedge, along with the inclusion of "we," captures the collaborative relationship of Jak to the others in relation to their task (planning), the tools at hand (ideas,

Excerpt 2.3 *Relational habitus structured as collaborative negotiations*

Jak:	I↑ think we should just- [>get seeds< =	2.29
Paige:	[that's it see::ds	2.30
Jak:	=cause that's [all wh (.) what all what all we want:↑	2.31
	[(((Pointing to a list of seeds written on*	2.32
	a sheet of paper on their table.))	2.33
Keith:	I ↑think that we should just	2.34
Lulu:	[choose- one:	2.35
	[(((Points to Jak.))*	2.36
Keith:	no- maybe we should all agree [on a couple	2.37
	[(((Nodding his head for*	2.38
	emphasis.))	2.39
Lulu:	HOW BOUT↑ use	2.40
Keith:	all agree on a couple	2.41
WA-	ok [so how can we do that *((Gentle voice.))*	2.42
Becca:	[(((Turns away from writing to look at Keith and Paige.))*	2.43
Keith:	all agree on a [couple	2.44
	[(((Leans in toward the paper where WA-Becca*	2.45
	is writing down their ideas.))	2.46
Lulu:	um::↓ do a vo:te↑	2.47
Jak:	wait wuh	2.48
Sarah:	wait everybody (.) wait one person picks one: (.) not-like-	2.49
	all	2.50
Lulu:	two or three or [four	2.51
Sarah:	[like one person picks one=	2.52
	[(((Moves to orient towards Lulu.))*	2.53
	=so like Lulubell really wanted to do catnip so I guess	2.54
	so we: won't do catnip cuz:: we >already agreed we weren't	2.55
	gunna< do: that	2.56
Paige:	how about each↑ of us chooses one thing to grow:: by	2.57
	ourselves↓ so we [could learn about the seeds↑	2.58
SH	[cuz dhat dhat would be really hard though	2.59
	be↓cause (.) woo-	2.60
Paige:	but each udder↓could help each udder↑ with- our (..)	2.61
Sarah:	*((Mockingly repeating Paige.))* each other can help each	2.62
	other↑	2.63
Paige:	how about each person choo::ses↑	2.64
WA-	°that wasn't very nice↓ (..)°	2.65
Becca:	*((Speaking to Sarah about mocking Paige.))*	2.66
Paige:	how bout each person chooses one and den↑ we can help	2.67
	each o:ther grow each of them↑	2.68
Sarah:	that's actually↑	2.69
Lulu:	[oo or maybe↑ we could we shu	2.70
WA-	I think Sarah was talking	2.71
Becca:		

Sarah:	u::m↓ actually↑ I was thinking that we (.) that each of us	2.72
	can like (.) we can take turns working on each one like if	2.73
	Lulubell picks catnip one day (.) I would help grow:: it	2.74
	an:: I'd see .what it's doing ↑, (.) then:: Keith↓ would >do	2.75
	it < then Paige↓ >would do it< then Jak would do it then:	2.76
	(.) Lulubell would start working on it↑	2.77
WA-	ok well(.) before we can talk about how: wer'e going: to pick	2.78
Becca:	↑ (.) why↑ don't we: think about our seed goals (. . .) k↑:	2.79

suggestions), and accepted modes of action (decisions are accomplished by "all"). Jak's repetition of "all" also marks collaboration as the preferred way to engage in planning, that is, an indicator of how to regulate engagement to make meaning. In effect, his directive is a proposal for co-regulation, a common pattern in this setting.

Keith enters the negotiation process by partially repeating Jak ("I ↑think that we should just") but quickly self-repairs to make a different suggestion, that is, the group "should all agree on a couple" of seeds (lines 2.37–2.39). Similar to Jak, Keith creates a directive for future action by utilizing the modal verb "should" combined with a hedge "maybe" and marks collaboration as the preferred way to engage by repeating "all agree" three times, (lines 2.37, 2.41, 2.44). These actions contribute to the development of an RH that sustains participants' collaborative relationships toward tools, task, and others. This relationship influences the linguistic resources children used to negotiate meaning, in this case, the meaning of what to consider for future actions. The response of the WA, Becca ("so how can we do that"), also sustains the collaborative relationships, as it enacts a request for collaborative inquiry. Becca's request reveals her relationship to the children as a mentor, one who is inquisitive about children's ideas and solutions to problems. Here, Becca's use of "we" and her gentle voice mitigate the power relations she has with the children by benefit of her institutional position (undergraduate), age, and experience. This subtle mitigation of power helps Becca inhabit a unique position (identity) in this context, namely she is both a mentor and a member of the group.

In relation to the solution of "picking one," Lulu first suggests choosing "one" and then having a "vote" to decide (line 2.47). Later, she suggests picking more than one, perhaps "two, three or four" (line 2.51). Her suggestions are not elaborated on but are interwoven throughout the interaction as bids to collaborate in the group's thinking. In this way, she is attempting to participate in collaborative decision-making through co-regulatory processes. Like Keith, Lulu also has the right (agency) to make bids for solution methods, even though she is one of the youngest participants. Lulu's and Keith's bids for participation illustrate how younger (or newer) members of The Web contributed to a localized RH that structured collaborative thinking and collaborative tool use as a normative or habitual (i.e., without reflection) way to engage in meaning-making through behavioral regulation.

Sarah and Paige, who are more experienced and older members of The Web, elaborate their own solutions, which consistently include linguistic resources marking collaborative negotiation/decision-making and collaborative actions as preferred. At the same time, Sarah and Paige indicate an expectation that individual members will self-regulate their behaviors. For example, Sarah begins her suggestion (line 2.49) in response to Keith with a strong command, "wait," which directs attention to her proposed solution that "one person picks <u>one</u>: (.) not- like- all." Sarah completes her contribution to the collaborative negotiation process at the end of the excerpt, when she uses linguistic resources similar to those of Jak and Keith, that is, a directive for future action combined with a hedge created by the cognitive verb to think ("I was thinking"). Sarah's elaborated solution reveals how the local RH emphasizes co-regulation of actions and thought in the form of socially shared regulation (or regulated by the group) as a means to achieve self-regulation. This happens when Sarah first indicates that each member can select a particular seed to grow with the help of another member ("if Lulubell picks catnip one day (.) I would help grow::"). Sarah's solution is a patterned way of engaging (lines 2.73–2.77), one that is also found in Paige's suggestion that each member chooses one seed to grow but also "help each udder↑." Here again, the RH that is emerging and being sustained creates a relationship among selves, tools, tasks, and others that fosters co-regulation as the primary means of achieving self-regulation for collaborative and socially shared regulation.

Ultimately, these children collaboratively researched and selected the seeds that would work best in their geographic location and would mature before the end of the semester. They worked together to plant, grow, and harvest their crop, learning about organic farming along the way. The processes of selecting, planting, and growing seeds mirrored Excerpt 2.3 in that the social organization of the local RH shaped regulatory processes such that self-regulation led to the continual emergence and maintenance of co-regulation (between individuals who negotiated meaning) and socially shared regulation (the whole group co-regulating the negotiation of meaning). The development and maintenance of this RH contributed to an ecological ensemble of relations where all members could regulate their behaviors to participate in generative, flexible, and creative thinking in relation to the task at hand, negotiate the meaning of tools, and propose problem solutions. In sum, The Web's local RH shaped a truly hybrid community where multiple and competing voices aligned in collaboration and became resources for each participant's learning and development.

Of course, the tasks presented by Mr. Minton and the Wiz could have been structured very differently. For example, if the presented problems were articulated as individual tasks in which students had to work alone, then the relationships between selves, tools, tasks, and others would have been different. They might have led to an emphasis on self-regulatory processes in which intersubjective interactions become oriented toward searches for correct responses rather than the negotiation of meaning. Such relationships might have been activated primarily by self-regulation. What this implies is the importance of consciously fostering the construction and development of a relational habitus that fosters productive and agential engagement in meaning-making through regulatory processes.

The examples presented in this chapter, particularly the playful learning context, illustrate how a carefully constructed RH makes it possible for the regulation of thinking and problem-solving to be distributed among all members, from novices to experts, to create an egalitarian learning community in which agency emerges as a relational process. Such communities do not preexist and they rarely happen by chance. On the contrary, they emerge from the way the RH is historically structured over time and from how the RH frames what a learner can do and cannot do, as well as what cognitive and practical actions are preferred. The relational habitus configures the existing context of intersubjective processes of meaning-making; it also shapes behavior in context or anticipates a new context for these processes. The structuring of relational rights and responsibilities can be thought of as a cultural process of context building. In this dynamic process, all participants – whether learners, teachers, mentors, parents, and so on – are active contributors and all of them influence the construction and development of the sociocultural frame through which regulatory processes take shape.

CHAPTER 3

Practical-Moral Knowledge
and Regulatory Processes

In this chapter, we introduce a theoretical framework for practical-moral knowledge (PMK), an important contextual influence on learners' engagement in regulatory processes during routine learning. PMK is a locally situated and co-constructed form of knowledge that brings a moral valence to the psychological and pragmatic actions and interactions used to regulate meaning-making behaviors. In fact, learners and their mentors consistently use PMK to coordinate their attention, responses, and actions during joint activities. This means that PMK is always involved in the task accomplishment occurring via relational intersubjective processes of knowledge construction, that is, within a *relational habitus*. Yet there is scant research on how this form of cultural knowledge (re)emerges as a directive resource for behavioral regulation in learning contexts (see Shotter, 1993). Here, we offer a theoretical frame for PMK as well as data-based examples to illustrate how it can be used as an analytical tool for observing and explaining contextual variances in the ways that learners regulate their behaviors.

There is no doubt that controlling intellectual and pragmatic engagement in complex cognitive activities is a widely recognized form of competency across multiple disciplines, one that leads to productive and successful engagement in effective learning (Dent & Koenka, 2016; Panadero, 2017; Zheng, 2016). The development of this competency, however, does not occur in "neutral" arenas of learning. Rather, it emerges from participation in everyday learning activities in which community members draw from knowledge construction interactions/actions that are locally deemed morally right, desired, and legitimate. As learners construct and then utilize their understandings of these moral aspects of their social context, they draw from their interpretations and comprehensions of PMK. This form of knowledge acts as a sign system (tool) or contextual resource for determining how to regulate behavior during the uncertainties and ambiguities of learning activities. In learning arenas,

PMK functions as a locally constructed directive form of tacit (unarticulated) knowledge because it emerges from two forms of implicit aspects of social contexts: social and moral orders.

Social Order: Implicit and Emergent

Social order in learning communities arises from implicit understandings about how to (properly) get things done in routine activity. This can vary quite a bit between settings; for example, learners may apply different "rules" depending on whether they are asking questions in peer-group work or in formal teacher-directed lessons. Through their sustained participation in a community of practice, learners come to understand emergent situational differences for knowledge construction, or what Garfinkel (1967) calls "background expectancies" for who can do what, when, and how. The enactment of these background expectancies over interactional time is the form of practical knowledge used to create and enact the *social order* of a learning context. For example, when students use directives such as commands (e.g., "just do it this way"), as a form of other-regulation to enact help-giving, they are most likely drawing from their understanding of background expectancies for how to engage in knowledge construction with others. Later, learners may begin to use a different set of strategies if or when they discover that suggestions and questions (i.e., co-regulation) lead to more desirable outcomes. When learners change the practical actions that they use to give help, they are acting agentially to create different interactional and relational patterns for constructing knowledge collaboratively. Through these actions, they are potentially transforming background expectancies along with concomitant pragmatic actions to engage in learning activity. In other words, learners are regulating their behavior to instantiate and potentially transform social order. Accordingly, social order in learning areas is the maintenance of common intellectual, behavioral, and relational patterns for constructing knowledge both individually and collaboratively. Because social order comes into existence over interactional time (i.e. it occurs in the present and is influenced by past interactions), it is both an emergent phenomenon and an historical resource that learners can draw from. Consequently, practical knowledge and social order are mutually constitutive.

Social order emerges from a dynamic interrelationship between two aspects of practical knowledge: background expectancies of who can do what, when, where, and how (an unpackaging of the division of labor in

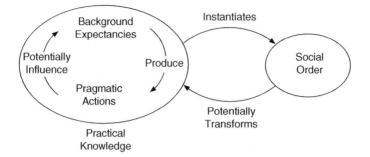

Figure 3.1   Emergence of social order: tacit background expectancies of who can do
what, when, where, and how

the cultural-historical activity theory (CHAT) model, first mentioned in
Chapter 1; see Figure 1.4); and the transformation of these expectancies
into the pragmatic (regulated) actions used to accomplish learning activities in the moment and over time (Figure 3.1). This is a nonlinear process
as the unfolding of learning activities always involves a dynamic process of
transactions between individuals and their environment. In turn, these
transactions give rise to emergent ways of doing, being, and learning in
particular contexts. Consequently, practical knowledge about how to
engage in learning activity is continually negotiated, renegotiated, and
potentially transformed as learners both draw from and contribute to
local background expectancies of how to get things done. Furthermore,
as practical knowledge is generated, learners respond opportunistically and
creatively to the exigencies of ongoing activity and, in doing so, they create
new situations for engagement. This ongoing interactive construction of
learning situations is the reason for the dynamic relationship between
background expectancies and pragmatic actions. In this way, social order
is never static. Rather, social order is in a bi-directional relationship with
the ever-changing practical knowledge of learners (and their mentors or
teachers). The potential transformation of how things get done is not
a neutral process because social order is linked to a second form of implicit
contextual understandings about engaging in a learning practice: moral
order.

Moral Order: Implicit and Emergent

Moral order, in relation to regulatory processes, emerges from implicit
understandings about a learning community's taken-for-granted values,

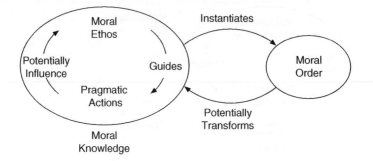

Figure 3.2   Emergence of moral order: local semiotic system of rights, responsibilities, and duties for engagement

beliefs, norms, and expectations for what is desirable, preferred, good, and right for engagement in knowledge construction. This is referred to as the moral ethos of a community. In effect, a community's moral ethos is a local semiotic system of rights, responsibilities, and duties that establishes legitimate cognitive and affective actions and interactions for competent participation. When learners draw on a community's moral ethos and take up the obligation and responsibility to utilize the preferred tools, signs, and social acts of knowledge construction, they are instantiating moral order. Similar to social order, moral order is both a historical resource and an emergent phenomenon that learners use to construct moral knowledge about competent engagement in their local community. How this process unfolds over interactional and historical time is shown in Figure 3.2.

Moral order emerges from a dynamic interrelationship between two aspects of moral knowledge: a community's moral ethos and those actions that bring this ethos into existence to accomplish learning activities (Figure 3.2). The selection of actions and interactions for engagement is guided by implicit, taken-for-granted beliefs about what is preferred and morally desirable for engagement. Consequently, learners' decisions to other-regulate (e.g., by issuing directives) or co-regulate (e.g., by making suggestions and/or asking questions) are guided by a community's moral ethos as well as those pragmatic acts and interactions used to instantiate that ethos. All the while, such decisions occur in the flurry of contingent and unpredictable social interactions that make up routine learning activities. In these contextual circumstances, learners can react creatively and opportunistically; consequently, moral order – like social order – is never static. Rather, it emerges from a dynamic relationship between a community's moral ethos and the pragmatic, agentive, spontaneous, and creative actions that learners use to instantiate that ethos.

So far, we have explained how practical and moral orders emerge from and are instantiated in routine learning activities. Now, we turn to the ways in which social and moral orders are woven together over interactional and historical time, with both becoming constituents of PMK (Figure 3.3).

Through the bidirectional and dynamic processes that produce PMK, the social organization of the pragmatic actions and interactions of learning is underpinned by local indices of legitimate actions, competent participation, and moral obligations for constructing knowledge in particular ways. Yet social and moral orders for knowledge construction are rarely explicit. Rather, they are grounded in the emergent discursive practices of meaning-making that implicitly socialize learners into the local semiotic system of rights, responsibilities, and duties for regulating behavior. Accordingly, through the meaning-making processes that foster psychological and social-emotional development, social and moral orders become the interwoven constituents of contextually situated and constructed PMK. Importantly, PMK influences participants' decisions about how to regulate their intellectual, affective, and pragmatic behaviors in ways that are congruent with the social and moral orders of their local learning community.

As shown in Figure 3.3, three common patterns of behavioral regulation are influenced by PMK: self-, other-, and co-regulation. All three forms of regulation can be found in all learning communities. What is more, when learners enter a new community, they bring prior PMK to bear on how they regulate their engagement in that environment. Prior understandings of PMK will, in turn, be influenced and potentially transformed by the emergent learning practices of the new community. As a consequence, patterns in PMK may vary from one learning arena to another.

To illustrate how regulatory processes relate to the construction of PMK in a learning community, we share examples taken from two of the author's video ethnographies of literacy teaching and learning. These examples come from two separate classrooms in the same urban school located in northern California. The classrooms share similarities in their student populations but are characterized by quite different instructional practices. As we will show, different forms of PMK emerge, resulting in differently patterned variations of behavioral regulation.

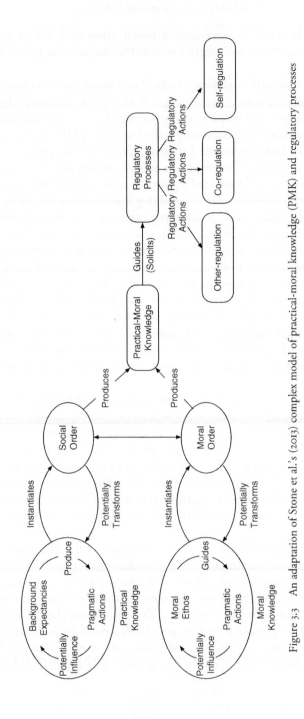

Figure 3.3 An adaptation of Stone et al.'s (2013) complex model of practical-moral knowledge (PMK) and regulatory processes

Toggle Pattern of Shifts: Other-Regulation and Self-Regulation

The first set of examples comes from the classroom of Ms. S, whose instructional practices are "traditional" in the sense that teacher-directed lessons position instructors as the primary managers of engagement, the primary evaluators and arbiters of accurate interpretations of information, and the primary source of knowledge construction strategies. In her own words, Ms. S characterized her instructional approach as a "mission" to help students "learn and think." Accordingly she organized her lessons by presenting problems and structuring engagement as a stepwise progression of task completion, often incorporating worksheets as key tools with obligatory requests to follow teacher-generated procedures. A focus on correctness, the efficient use of time, and on-task behaviors were all knowledge construction strategies that we frequently observed in her classroom.

To show how Ms. S fostered a toggle pattern of regulation where she used other-regulation as the primary way for learners to self-regulate, we offer two excerpts taken from a literacy lesson. This particular lesson, which focused on a historical fiction book, *Valley of the Moon: The Diary of Maria Rosalia de Miagros*, was intended to assist students in developing strategies for recognizing and identifying sensory images (e.g., hearing, seeing, smelling), which they would then use to complete an assignment. Both excerpts illustrate how locally instantiated social and moral orders foster PMK, which, in turn, structured students' engagement in the learning activity. Here, a distinct toggle pattern of other-regulation to self-regulation is evident.

In Excerpt 3.1, Ms. S is reading the task directions aloud to her students. She makes explicit the need to listen before writing (lines 3.16–20) so that she can highlight the importance of "thinking" about what the task requires. Ms. S also lists the five senses and links them to "sensory images."

As Ms. S initiates problem articulation, she begins to establish herself as a manager (other-regulator) of engagement. This continues as she uses polite but explicit directives to position herself as the other-regulator of behavior, such as "I want you to . . ." (lines 3.22, 3.39) and "I would like you to . . ." (line 3.18). She also uses other-regulation to mark efficiency as necessary and desirable through the use of a time-focused directive, ">one two three tell me<," (line 3.30). The students, in turn, self-regulate to produce a correct response, "<hearing>" (line 3.31). Ms. S then positively evaluates that response, as "°okay° . . . >okay<" (line 3.32). Next, Ms. S describes behaviors (i.e., strategies) for solving the problem. For example, "sort and classify in your head" is emphasized as necessary forms of self-

Excerpt 3.1 *Problem articulation: valuing other-regulation*

Ms. S:	*((Standing at the front of the class with book in hand.))*	3.10
	. . . <we are going to be looking > fo::r some: sensory images	3.11
	so would you please f↑i::nd your sensory image pa:ge . . .	3.12
	Arright . this says look for descriptions that involve the five	3.13
	senses such as the the wind whispered: through the trees (1.0)	3.14
	or the smell of fre<u>sh</u>ly baked bread filled the house . write an	3.15
	example from the book for <u>each</u> of the senses include the page	3.16
	number for refere<u>nce</u> (.) alright:: <u>now</u> be↑fo:re we start (.)	3.17
	doing anything with this sheet for (.) to↑day's ↓pages (.) ↑I	3.18
	would ↑like you (4.1) to g↑o::: >you're <u>not</u> going to be wri-<	3.19
	↑are you gonna be writing on the sheet right now for[-	3.20
Class:	[no::::	3.21
Ms. S:	no I just want you to th<u>ink</u> ↑about <u>hearing smelling seeing</u>	3.22
	<u>tasting feeling</u> those are the senses that we're looking for those	3.23
	are the <↑<u>sensory images</u>> we're looking for (2.6) ↑first of	3.24
	a::ll (2.2) the wind whispered through the trees <↑what sense>	3.25
	is ↑th↓at	3.26
Class:	*((Multiple students raise hands.))*	3.27
Ms. S:	that's what we would call uh sensory image what sense do you	3.28
	u::<u>se</u> <to know that the wind whi<u>sp</u>ered through the trees>	3.29
	>one two three tell me<	3.30
Class:	<hearing>	3.31
Ms. S:	°okay° . . . >okay< so ↑what you have to ↓do:: (1.6) is sort and	3.32
	classify in your h↑ead (3.4) thing one it's uh like uh	3.33
	↓flowchart ↑question (1) <u>does</u> this paint a picture in my mind	3.34
	↑if ↑y::es (2) well if no:: <then just move ↑right> (1.8) yes it's	3.35
	more complicated here (3.5) ↑if ↑ye::s (.) then you have to	3.36
	a::<u>sk</u> (9) what sen↑se (2.4) >an how do I kn- or< yeah you	3.37
	have to ask what sen↑se (5.2) °and then you have to de↑cide	3.38
	(5.5) aright (1.2) what I ↑want you to ↓do ↑is flip back	3.39
	through the pages that we've <u>al</u>::ready read flip back through	3.40
	the pages that we've <u>al::ready read</u> (1.4) <and ↑you:: are going	3.41
	to be looking ↓fo::r> ≪A SENSORY IMAGE≫ you can	3.42
	work with the person next to you you are looking for A	3.43
	SENSORY IMAGE	3.44
	((Students begin working and talking))	3.45
Ms. S:	just waituh- how many is A::: ↓sensory ↓image how many	3.46
	is ↑that	3.47
Class:	[one	3.48
Ms. S:	[<u>one</u> so you need to know what the words of the passage ↑are	3.49
	you need to know (what page it's on so we can find it so we	3.50
	can read it ↑too) and you need to know what sense	3.51

regulation (lines 3.32–3.35) through the use of obligatory directives produced like, "what you have to [do]," (lines 3.32, 3.36–3.37, 3.39) and "you need to know . . ." (lines 3.49–3.51). In this way, while Ms. S positions herself as a manager, she marks other-regulation as the preferred and desirable route to self-regulation.

Later in the same lesson, Ms. S asks students to share examples of sensory images that they have found in their book. The next excerpt begins as she requests an example of "tasting." A student, Chase, shares his example, which is based on an inference about taste rather than a description of it (lines 3.60–3.62). Once again, in this interactional event, Ms. S positions herself as a source of information and the arbiter of correct knowledge.

Ms. S initially accepts Chase's example but then hesitates, ultimately rejecting it with an evaluation, "don't know really what it tas:tes like" (line 3.69). She then goes on to use a think-aloud strategy to model how to think about and evaluate a similar example (lines 3.71–3.82). In this classroom, Ms. S's own think-alouds positioned her as a provider of information and ultimately as an evaluator of it. This modeling also functioned as a way for children to learn and then employ the same (other-regulated) strategy to self-regulate their engagement in learning.

As Ms. S completes this modeling, another student, Sara, evaluates Chase's example ("but you kinda know what it tastes like" lines 3.84, 3.88–3.90), claiming that the evaluation "best . . . ever" could, in fact, be used to make an inference about taste. Further, Sara is making a bid to co-regulate by negotiating an alternative view as to whether Chase's example counts as a tasting sensory image. Ms. S rejects Sara's claim as well as Sara's bid for co-regulation by sharing her evaluation of the example as a feeling ("this one might have been more of uh fee:ling," lines 3.92–3.94). Another student, Ellie, evaluates Ms. S's example by claiming that an inference could be made about taste through the action of nibbling ("they nibbled at it"). Ms. S's response is another rejection as she reiterates her earlier evaluation, "well that's uh feeling now isn't it" (line 3.99).

In this classroom, Ms. S typically positioned herself as the primary arbiter of correctness and the primary other-regulator of learning. Students were expected to engage in thinking, problem-solving, and finding correct responses; that is, they were expected to act agentially to self-regulate their behavior in response to other-regulation by the teacher, thereby engaging in a toggle pattern of other- to self-regulation. These children were not, however, expected to engage in the negotiation of meaning, that is, co-regulation. Because self-regulation was initiated through other-regulation, and because bids for co-regulation were rejected

Excerpt 3.2 *The toggle pattern: other-regulation to self-regulation*

Ms. S:	a:right↑ [so did any- uh >did any one↑< finduh↑=	3.52
	[((*Looks from one table to another.*))	3.53
	=tas↓ting↑ (3.0)	3.54
	Chase [≫what'd you fine↓what page↑ ≪	3.55
	[((*Gestures toward Chase with hand.*))	3.56
Chase:	page↑ twenty↑ two↓	3.57
Ms. S:	[page twenty↑ two:	3.58
	[((*Lifts up book closer to face. Flips through pages.*))	3.59
Chase:	((*Reading from book.*))	3.60
	Señor Johnson slath↑ered the piece of butter then	3.61
	proclaimed it was the best he'd ever eaten↓	3.62
Ms. S:	[ar::ight (1.7)	3.63
	[((*Looks at Chase and then at book.*))	3.64
	so:↓ he: uhm (.)so we- don↑okay	3.65
	he'd proclaimed [it was the best he'd ever eaten >but we=	3.66
	[((*Looks up from book.*))	3.67
	= don't know really < what it tas:tes like (.)	3.68
	[but I was think↑ing↑ <tha::t uhm(.)=	3.69
	[((*Looks down at book.*))	3.70
	=that [that would be uh tas↑ting↓>	3.71
	[((*Looks up.*))	3.72
	= (1.0)°cause I remember° they did taste it that that	3.73
	[((*Looks down to read from book.*))	3.74
	[the Medinas politely ni↑bbled at it and paid	3.75
	compliments[but I know they =	3.76
	[((*Glances up from book.*))	3.77
	= did [not care for it °didn't like the taste° but it =	3.78
	[((*Looks up, nodding her head.*))	3.79
	= >doesn it's [not really describing	3.80
	[((*Slightly moving head side to side.*))	3.81
	the tas-it's not telling us what it tastes like↑<	3.82
	((*Looking at the class.*))	3.83
Sara:	°but you kinda know↓what↑ it tastes like°	3.84
	((*Sitting close by to the right of Mrs. S.*))	3.85
Ms. S:	[wha::t↑	3.86
	[((*Turns and looks at Sara.*))	3.87
Sara:	you kinda↑ know↓ what it tastes like [cauz (inaudible)	3.88
	[((*Turns head	3.89
	and points to Chase.*))	3.90
Ms. S:	[okay ((*Looks	3.91
	at book.*)) so this one↑ okay so [this one might have =	3.92
	[((*Looks at Sara.*))	3.93
	= been more of a fee:ling ((*Looks toward Ellie's table.*))	3.94
	(2.5) Ell↑ie↓ >what were you gonnta↑ say↓ [what page↑<	3.95

Ellie: [uhm I↑ was   3.96
          gonna uhm say the Medinas tried that they nibbled at it   3.97
          [(unclear)   3.98
Ms. .:   [okay↑ okay↑ [well that's uh feeling now isn't it   3.99
                       [((Tilts head slightly to one side then nods 3.100
                          head.))   3.101

by Ms. S, her directions to students to "talk it over" or "work together" did not generally result in students utilizing co-regulation. Instead, students in this classroom engaged in self-regulation and other-regulation through issuing directives to each other. Interestingly, these children other-regulated one another's engagement even when Ms. S was not co-present in a conversation. For example, when unsanctioned strategies or information were used, it was common for students to engage in other-regulation, for example directing one another that, ">You have to use< one of tho: se (.) words" or "we're not allowed to use it." In this learning context, students came to privilege an individual search for correct responses and the prevalent use of other-regulation as a means of collaborating. In other words, when students enacted other-regulation as the primary means to assist each other in dyadic and small-group interactions, they were using PMK. Simultaneously, they were instantiating the local social and moral order as shifts between other- and self-regulation.

Dynamic Shifting Pattern: Co-Regulation to Self-Regulation

The next excerpts show how the construction of PMK in another classroom setting resulted in a strikingly different pattern of regulatory processes. These data come from the classroom of Mr. Minton a teacher whose instructional practices are best characterized as *social constructivist* with a strong emphasis on social interaction, collaboration, negotiation, and the use of cognitive tools. Mr. Minton positioned himself neither as the primary manager of engagement nor as the primary evaluator of understanding or knowledge construction. Rather, he established himself as someone who collaborated with others to seek solutions and who, at times, shared his expertise as a resource. Mr. Minton summed up his approach when he explained that, "One of the things I try to do is to figure out ways that I can ask questions that will get [the students] to discover the answers rather than me" (Stone, et al., 2013). To this end, Mr. Minton presented problems and posed questions oriented toward collaborative meaning-making. With this

Excerpt 3.3 *Problem articulation: co-regulation to self-regulation*

Mr. M:	((*Looking at the class from the front of the room.*))	3. 102
	write it and as you're writing it talk it over with each other	3.103
	s::ee if you can come up with (.) where those accents might	3.104
	go (.) so write it down first (.) say it to yourself and the::n	3.105
	see what you think talk it over with each other . . . all we're	3.106
	trying to do is to see:: (.) which of the syllables are accented	3.107
	more heavily (.) and if we can see that then we can <pull the	3.108
	pattern> that the poet is using °out of the poem° . . . this	3.109
	information can transfer to your ability to be able to write in	3.110
	a pattern (1.5) cause that's where you want to be >if you	3.111
	were writing a poem< and you wanted to ↑fit a pat↓tern (.)	3.112
	you first get a sense of how is your poet's poem starting out	3.113
	what pattern is it ↑start↓ing with (.) and then you can make	3.114
	the rest of the poetry °fit that pattern°.	3.115

approach, students could then generate their own solutions, methods, interpretations, and/or understandings of the presented problems. This created a classroom culture where information and knowledge construction emerged from negotiated or co-regulatory processes. Here, actions such as teacher–student and peer–peer help-giving and help-seeking, informal discussions/negotiations, and prior experiences were all considered necessary for knowledge construction.

The following data come from one of Mr. Minton's poetry lessons, the purpose of which was to help students understand the role of accented syllables in poetry. Later on, students would be expected to self-regulate their behavior by using this knowledge to create poems of their own. Three excerpts follow. In the first (Excerpt 3.3), Mr. Minton initiates the presented problem by explaining the task at hand, namely the students must read a line from a poem written on the front board ("Jimmy Jet") and identify a pattern. (Note, in the transcript, Mr. Minton is referred to as Mr. M.)

In presenting the problem, Mr. M begins with a directive ("write it") followed by utterances that are co-regulatory, framing students as collaborative agents in thinking and communicating about problem solutions. With his communication, Mr. M sets up expectations that students co-regulate their engagement with others and self-regulate individually, using directives like, "talk it over with each other" (lines 3.102–3.103). What is more, Mr. M uses "we" to describe what needs to be done ("all we're trying to do is to see:: (.) which of the syllables are accented more heavily," and "if we can see that then we can <pull the pattern> that the poet is using °out of the poem°"). While the use of the inclusive "we" could be interpreted as a bid by

Excerpt 3.4 *Marking collaboration and negotiation as valuable*

Ricky:	*((Standing next to Mr. M at the front of the room.))*	3.116
	I was just wondering: (.) is this one of those thing::s: where::.	3.117
	um there is one right way to do it. where [it's just use	3.118
Mr. M:	[no. no (.)	3.119
	well in certain types of poetry you will see. that there	3.120
	will be one right, way to do it. all I want you to do is to,	3.121
	f::i:nd a pa:ttern (..) a::nd when you f::ind that pattern	3.122
	realize the pa:ttern [is ther:e, so that when you're writing	3.123
	your =	3.124
Alise:	[*((Sits back in her chair with her foot on*	3.125
	the seat, knee up and elbow resting on the chair's back. Her	3.126
	cheek rests in her hand as she looks at the teacher.))	3.127
Mr. M:	=>own poetry< you can see if you could make it fit, the same	3.128
	pattern. so I will recognize that there's different people who	3.129
	can see: this different ways now, some poetry I'll show you	3.130
	that that it follows a ↓real strict pattern. so let's try this. the	3.131
	third poem	3.132
	((reading from front board))	3.133
	I'll tell you a story of Jimmy Jett and you'll know what I tell	3.134
	[you is true.=	3.135
Alise:	[°I'll t:ell you. the st:ory. I'll tell you the story of Jim:::°	3.136
	[*((Moves her hand from her check to cover her*	3.137
	mouth as she simultaneously begins private talk while	3.138
	looking at Mr. M and Ricky standing at the front board.))	3.139

Mr. M to other-regulate in the form of a polite directive, in this setting it functions more as a request to co-regulate and includes Mr. M as a co-participant. Here, problem-solving involves "figuring [things] out" rather than following specified procedures. Not unexpectedly, Mr. M's list of pragmatic actions for knowledge production typically involved actions for both co- and self-regulation. For example, Mr. M shifts from collaborative to self-regulatory behaviors when he tells the students that they can "transfer" or appropriate their new knowledge to write a poem (lines 3.104, 3.109–112). This agential framing of students explains why co-regulation was marked as a preferred and desired form of engagement in this classroom. Consequently, when students took up these actions to construct literacy understandings, they were using their PMK of how to engage in meaning-making, thereby instantiating the local social and moral order.

Excerpt 3.4 captures an event that occurred a few minutes later in the same lesson. It illustrates Mr. M's positive stance toward co-regulation as well as the framing of students as active agents in regulatory processes. In this excerpt, a learner (Ricky) gets up from his group and goes to the front of the class to initiate a tentative request to Mr. M to share his reflections on a topic (lines 3.116–3.118). Another student, Alise, remains with her small group but self-regulates her behavior to attend to the interactions between Mr. M and Ricky.

Ricky's question ("I was just wondering: (.) is this one of those thing::s: where::, um there is one right way to do it. where it's just use") was a revoicing of the typical ways in which Mr. M himself framed the act of understanding, that is, as being curious or thoughtful about an idea or topic not yet fully grasped. This approach to understanding contributed to the local indices of legitimate actions and competent participation by positioning students as collaborative meaning-makers or co-regulators in the sense that meaning emerged from a relational process of communal grappling for understanding. In this classroom, this learning strategy became an expected part of knowledge construction as well as the community's ethos for regulating learning behaviors. Students' uptake of this approach helped instantiate both social and moral order and also served as a display of their PMK for regulating learning behaviors with questions, ideas, and uncertainties.

Mr. M's stance on involving others in the process of meaning-making was also enacted by his habitual positioning of students as actors who could select from a range of possibilities and resources. This was accomplished in part by Mr. M's use of conditionals to imply possibility in future actions – for example, "you can see if you could make it fit." He frequently combined such conditional constructions with modal verbs of desire (e.g., "if you're willing to . . . you could . . .," or "if you wanted to . . . you could"). His use of these grammatical constructions positioned students as self-regulated agents who could evaluate, select, and determine whether and how to engage in learning activities. That is, local PMK resulted in a community ethos in which students expected to be managers and arbiters of the preferred pragmatic actions used to self- and/or co-regulate behavior during meaning-making events.

An example of how students managed these regulatory actions over interactional time is seen in Excerpt 3.4 when Alise oriented herself away from her three-member peer group and toward the conversation between Mr. M and Ricky (lines 3.125–3.127). Alise used private speech to self-regulate (line 3.136) when she covered her mouth and whispered, yet she continued to gaze at the teacher. Alise's private speech, which overlapped with Mr. M's utterances, indicates self-directed behavior through the imitation of the teacher's utterances (see Stone & Hart, 2007). In fact, in this classroom setting, it was common for the students to self-regulate by shifting their attention away from their small groups to overhear and draw from other student–teacher conversations. They would then use this resource to co-regulate by shifting back to their group to build (new) understandings. Such shifts were interwoven in collaborative activity as students drew from local PMK to regulate their behavior and, in effect, instantiate social and moral order.

Excerpt 3.5 shows how PMK could lead to dynamic shifts between self-, other-, and co-regulation. It begins as Alise realigns with her group and draws from different resources (her notes on syllables and her classmate's knowledge) to understand accented syllables in a particular line of poetry that was written on the front board: "My father was the first to hear the passing of the geese each year."

As Alise shifts from self-regulated private speech to face-to-face participation, she creates an opportunity for co-regulation with her peers, Nerses and Emily. Specifically, Alise initiates verbal engagement by saying, "I: do-n't get this:" (line 3.142) while glancing around the table. This produces an implicit help-seeking request, which is an expected way of initiating co-regulation in this classroom. Through her request, Alise positions herself as a novice, at least in the understanding of syllabic stress. Simultaneously, she positions her interlocutors as relative experts and as possible help givers. This interpersonal positioning of agency gives Alise's peers the rights to use resources to assist her, that is, to co-regulate their goal-directed activity.

The ways in which Alise's peers respond provide evidence of how local PMK results in the fluid movement between self-, other-, and co-regulatory processes. Alise's positioning bid is immediately taken up by Nerses and Emily, although in different ways. Nerses participates by acknowledging Alise's indirect request for help by glancing at her and then at Emily (line 3.143). Emily aligns with Alise by agreeing ("ah yeah") and evaluating syllabic stress as "weird." This combination of speech acts displays Emily's agreement that syllabic stress is difficult to understand and also implies that Alise's implicit request for help is reasonable. This acknowledgment works to soften the immediate obligatory directive (and strategy) proffered by Emily: "you just have to say it like like (.) my fa:: ther::" (lines 3.144–3.145). This softening of a directive serves a similar function as Mr. M's attenuation of his authority toward evaluating knowledge production (see Excerpt 3.4). For this reason, Emily's directive is a bid to other-regulate, but it is a hedged bid. By hedging, she is both providing a strategy and aligning with Alise as a collaborator in the participant role of

Excerpt 3.5 *The dynamic pattern of self-, co-, and other-regulation*

Alise:	((*Puts her hand down from her mouth, turns and leans into*	3.140
	the group. Glances quickly around the table.))	3.141
	I: do↑n't get this:	3.142
Nerses:	((*Looks up from his writing and looks at Alise and Emily.*))	3.143
Emily:	((*To Alise.*)) ah yeah, it's weird. you just have to say it like	3.144
	like (.) my ↑fa::ther::	3.145
Alise:	((*Looks rapidly between Emily and her notebook while Emily*	3.146
	is talking.))	3.147
Nerses:	((*Looking up and smiling.*))	3.148
Alise:	((*Laughs.*)) my ↑fa::ther::= ((*Sing-song voice, smiling,*	3.149
	moving her body in a rhythmic motion with her talk. Looks	3.150
	towards the front of the class then briefly at her notebook and	3.151
	then back up to Emily.))= [was. the ↑f::irst: to hear °ok°	3.152
Emily	[the firs:t	3.153
Alise:	what if you didn't say it like that. (hhh.)	3.154
	((*Alise's gaze shifts rapidly between Emily and Austin several*	3.155
	times as she asks this question.))	3.156
Emily	yeah you just have ta[	3.157
Alise:	((*giggling*)) [not everyone goes my [↑fa::ther::	3.158
	[((*Raises her*	3.159
	eyebrows and shifts her shoulders upward.))	3.160
Emily:	[I know you just have ta. (..)=	3.161
Nerses:	[((*Nerses looks up from this paper toward the group. He*	3.162
	smiles widely and laughs slightly.))	3.163
Alise:	[((*Alise looks back to her notebook.*))	3.164
Emily:	=you just have ta[=	3.165
Nerses:	[I am your fa::th::er:	3.166
	((*In a low voice-imitating Darth Vader, then returns to*	3.167
	working in his notebook.))	3.168
Alise:	((*Laughs.*)) ((*Reads from the board to the group.*))	3.169
	I'll tell you the story of Jimmy Jet and you'll know what I tell	3.170
	you is true. I didn't see >any [accent!<	3.171
	[((*Accentuates "accent"*	3.172
	with a quick hand gesture.))	3.173
	Can somebody help me with this?	3.174
	((*Glances around the group beginning with Nerses and*	3.175
	ending with Austin. She returns gaze to middle of table and	3.176
	waits for a response.))	3.177

help giver. Meanwhile, Nerses engages in a humorous way, drawing from pop culture and imitating the voice of the Star Wars character Darth Vader to exaggerate syllabic stress ("I am your fa::th::er:", line 3.166). Again, these students instantiated the social order of collaborative knowledge construction, which relied on the implied expectation that negotiated knowledge was legitimate and preferred, that is, the community's moral ethos.

Alise laughs as she revoices Emily's strategy for figuring out syllabic stress ("my fa::ther::"). This is an uptake of Emily's strategy and evidence of the shift to co-regulation. After reading the line of poetry from the board, Alise suddenly asks a hypothetical question, "what if you didn't say it like that" (line 3.154) as she looks to the members of her small group, which is another initiation of co-regulation. Her question leads Emily to repeatedly offer an imperative to pronounce "father" in a particular way: ("you just have ta" lines 3.144, 3.157, 3.161, 3.165). The use of imperative grammatical constructions or obligatory directives has been found to close down talk in learning events and call for action over reflection (see Wagner & Herbel-Eisenmann, 2008). However, this is not the case in this interaction. Instead, Alise continues to pursue the problem of figuring out accented syllables when she explicitly asks for help while glancing at her group members: "can somebody help me with this?" (line 3.174). Other-regulation in the form of obligatory directives was not common in this classroom or in Mr. M's instructional discourse; instead, modal constructions were preferred. Thus, when obligatory directives did not lead to understanding they were rejected in favor of co-regulation. The continual search for understanding was based in the PMK of the community and, in this setting, precluded the primacy of other-regulation for knowledge construction.

The common pattern found in Mr. M's class involved students persistently pursuing understanding by interacting with others, requesting help even in the face of difficulties. This pursuit relied on local PMK as well as what constituted an accepted intellectual tool. Mr. M consistently used linguistic resources, such as modal verbs of possibility (could, might, would), to position students as agents who could determine for themselves what available resources to use and how. In fact, the use of a variety of resources was seen as competent, desirable, and preferred for the construction of knowledge in this setting (moral knowledge).

Taken as a whole, the data from Mr. M's classroom reveal how the PMK in this context emerged from collaboration and negotiation being marked as the preferred and desired way to engage in knowledge construction. This preference, which involved both social order and moral order, resulted in a semiotic system of rights and responsibilities that required shared agency and responsibility for assessing and constructing knowledge by both teacher and students. What we saw in Mr. M's classroom was dynamically shifting patterns of self-, other-, and co-regulation, with the local PMK of this classroom influencing the ways in which students engaged in the regulatory processes of meaning-making.

Influences of PMK on Behavioral Regulation

Vygotsky (1934/1986) argued that to explain meaning-making, the catalyst of higher mental functions, "we must uncover the means by which man learns to organize and direct his behavior" (p. 102). In other words, regulatory processes are essential to human development. This chapter on PMK illustrates the role that learning contexts play in this process. We suggest that patterns of engagement in intra- and inter-mental behavioral regulation are related to PMK – specifically, how it is constructed and how it emerges from social and moral order. In our model, the background expectancies that inform the pragmatics of learning become constitutive of the local social order. Further, we contend that the pragmatic actions of social order are guided by a community's moral ethos or semiotic system of rights and obligations for regulating learning practices. Accordingly, the PMK of a community always emerges from a bidirectional relationship between social and moral order.

To describe how variance in social and moral order produces differences in PMK and, therefore, differences in patterns of regulation, we analyzed the learning practices of two classrooms. In one of these classrooms, the teacher, Ms. S, positioned herself as an information provider and an arbiter and evaluator of correctness, with a marked emphasis on efficiency. She positioned students as agents in constructing or finding correct answers and correctly using teacher-generated procedures efficiently. These practices resulted in the emergence of PMK that was used by students (and teacher) to structure their engagement as a toggle pattern between other-regulation and self-regulation, with little evidence of co-regulation. The emphasis on other-regulation as the way to achieve self-regulation created particular forms of agential actions as preferred, good, and morally right. These actions generally lead learners to regulate their behaviors to determine if they were engaging in learning the "right way" from the teacher's perspective rather than their own.

In another classroom, the teacher, Mr. M, mitigated the role of the teacher as arbiter of correctness by positioning himself along with his students as co-participants in evaluating understandings, that is, evaluating one's own thinking and that of others, a collective form of metacognition. To ensure that learners co-regulated learning, Mr. M emphasized the importance of negotiating incomplete or not yet fully grasped knowledge. Although Mr. M shared strategies and his knowledge during literacy lessons, his students were expected to decide which strategies were needed and/or most appropriate to negotiate and construct knowledge. In Mr. M's classroom, the students and teacher alike used their PMK to structure their engagement in a regulatory pattern of dynamic shifts between self-, other-, and co-regulation, with an emphasis on co-regulation. The emphasis on co-regulation as the preferred, good, and morally acceptable way to construct literacy knowledge routinely led learners to self- and co-determine if they were engaging in learning "the right" way.

Traditional psychological research focuses on an individual's development of self-regulation with little regard for how the moral aspects of social practices come to influence the development of self-regulated (voluntary/agential) control of our thoughts, feelings, and problem-solving actions and interactions. In contrast, our analytical frame conceptualizes regulatory processes as influenced by PMK. This form of knowledge emerges from a fundamentally relational process and is influenced by the ways participants engage in learning practices. Our relational framing suggests that regulatory processes originate not simply within the individual but rather through engagement in a community's learning practices. During this engagement, learners construct social and moral meanings and these meanings contribute to the emergence of a local semiotic (sign) system of rights, responsibilities, and duties for regulating behavior. Vygotsky (1966) argued that within learning practices "the child begins to practice with respect to himself the same forms of [moral and regulated] behavior that others formerly practiced with respect to him" (pp. 39–40). Because of this, in order to fully understand how children (or adults) learn to control and direct their psychological and practical behaviors in learning settings, it is necessary to examine the interrelationship between individuals and their sociocultural context without losing sight of the moral, social, and cognitive complexity of social practices. Our theoretical model of PMK provides a means to do just this by revealing how individuals' development and competent use of regulatory processes emerge from the co-construction of PMK within learning contexts.

CHAPTER 4

Identity and Competence Woven Together Through Regulatory Processes

[O]ur definition of competence shape[s] our identities through our very engagement in activities and social interaction.

Wenger (1998, p. 193)

This chapter offers *identity of competency* as an analytical frame that reconceptualizes competency as an emergent, situated, and implicitly inhabited social identity. This approach represents a growing recognition among social and cultural scholars that identity and competency become interwoven in the ongoing construction of a sociocultural context (Fields & Enyedy, 2013; Gee, 2000; Leander, 2002; Stone & Hart, 2002; Wenger, 1998). The analytical frame for identity in this chapter varies from the more common psychological approaches to identity as involving narratives of self or membership in a particular social group (e.g., ethnic, race, class, etc.) or a publicly achieved and recognized social group (e.g., athletes, reporters, dancers, etc.). Rather, we draw from sociocultural psychology and linguistic anthropology to frame identity as locally situated and semiotically mediated through discourse practices, or what is said and done with others (Holland & Lachicotte, 2007; Ochs, 1993, 1996). From this perspective, identity is one form of self-authoring that is dialogically co-constructed and inhabited by taking on the status roles of a social identity related to, valued by, and emerging in a local community of practice (Kockelman, 2006). The conceptual frame for identity in this chapter provides a tool for observing how identity and competency become interwoven in learning settings through regulatory behaviors accomplished by the social acts of agential learners.

As learners engage in routine activities, they are not simply constructing content knowledge; they are also vying to inhabit social *identities of competency* by regulating their behavior in particular ways. These valued identities, commonly abbreviated by such adjectives as "smart," "brainy," or "sharp" to describe a learner, create an *implicit form of social identity* that is intersubjectively accomplished through agentive actions and interactions with others. What is more, in learning situations, the positive framing of identities of competency as desirable, and perhaps enjoyable, entices learners to regulate their engagement with others in ways that reflect a local community's values and moral ethos of rights, responsibilities, and obligations for how to gain and display competency with others. Of course, through recurrent engagement in these same regulatory processes, learners not only accomplish an identity of competency but also become competent in constructing knowledge with others.

All social identities refer to relational ways of being in the cultural world and emerge from the interactional processes of social meaning-making, that is, within a relational habitus (Kockelman, 2006; Stone et al., 2012; Vygotsky, 1978). Through these intersubjective processes, individuals enact identities associated with a particular social group, one that is valued or seen as contributing by the larger community – for example, being an artist, a doctor, a student, or teacher. These are publicly shared and recognized forms of identities, that is, these forms of social identity are explicitly articulated. There are, however, implicit forms of social identity that are beginning to be recognized in research studies (Devos & Banaji, 2003). Although not explicitly articulated (publicly identified), implicit identities are nonetheless enacted as a locally recognizable and valued form of social identity that are usually related to a particular community of practice. For example, recent research is beginning to show that teachers also vie to inhabit implicit identities such as collaborators or learners (Cohen, 2008, 2010). This emergent research points to why both explicit and implicit social identities come to be inhabited across communities of practice.

An identity of competency is one of those social and relational ways of being that implicitly emerges from face-to-face interactions across learning communities, including home, school, and work. For example, it is common in classroom settings for some children to be recognized and accepted as being "bright" or "clever" or "intelligent" by skillfully and agentially regulating their behaviors with others to use those knowledge construction actions and interactions marked as being competent or knowledgeable. These learners are often viewed by teachers and peers as local embodied "models" of competency. Yet these learners are more than simply models. For others in the classroom, and ultimately for themselves, these learners are enacting a social identity of being competent and this identity, although implicit, is socially agreed on and shared through communicative interactions. Of import, in learning settings, this form of implicit identity is both desirable and valued. Consequently, learners tend to enact, or at least try to enact, all of those social acts and interactions that display being a competent learner in their community. For this reason, identities of competency play an important role during learning activities because they function as a proleptic sign system (future in the present) of being a competent learner. Put simply, vying to inhabit an identity of competency helps learners see themselves as competent in the present even when competency is still emerging.

Thus, identities of competency have an important contextual and directive influence on how and when learners decide to regulate (control and direct) their engagement to initiate and persist in complex, challenging, and, at times, ambiguous learning activities. This is made possible because striving and struggling to inhabit a social identity of competency solicits learners to attend to those behaviors that are associated with competency and use them to regulate their behaviors with others.

In this chapter, to explain how learners come to take on an identity of competency, we will first draw from the work of Paul Kockelman (2006) to define social identity and detail how it emerges from enacting situational *roles*, which are best thought of as statuses with rights and responsibilities for particular actions and interactions. Next, we will describe how regulating behaviors to engage in these actions and interactions are interrelated with identities of competency in learning arenas. To illuminate how identities of competency are dialogically co-constructed over interactional time, we will provide an explanation of how learners and mentors or teachers use the linguistic resource of *stancetaking* (a form of interactional evaluation and positioning) during the enactment of roles to inhabit an identity of competency. Finally, utilizing examples taken from both formal and informal learning contexts, we will show how these processes shape and are shaped by continuously shifting forms of behavioral regulation.

Social Identities: Explicit and Implicit

Social identities are inhabited or embodied representations (signs) of the *values* of a community; as such, social identities are always relational. For example, identifying oneself and enacting those behaviors associated with being an artist, psychologist, or doctor indexes (points to) larger cultural values for each of these professions and their contributions to society. In academic settings, teachers are associated with society's values for learning and knowledge. When individuals take up the social identity of teacher they are anchoring themselves to these societal values. Common social identities associated with learning such as learner, mentor, teacher, or professor are *explicit* in that they are socially and historically shared with relative agreement about them in the larger cultural community.

On the other hand, social identities can also be *implicit* in the sense that they may not be explicitly articulated. For example, children or adults in a classroom setting might not overtly announce that they are "competent" or "smart" or "capable." Instead, these learners would agentively utilize those actions and interactions for behavioral regulation that are inextricably linked to how competency is locally defined, which include the values, practical-moral knowledge, and expectations for knowing and doing associated with their learning community. Through this process, implicit identities of competency are overtly enacted with others. Yet this enactment tacitly points to or indexes a shared social category for competency. Through these indexical actions, learners become attached to the emergent social category of competency and through this attachment they inhabit this local identity. Consequently, implicit forms of identity can vary across communities, each of which may have its own local beliefs, values, and practices pertaining to what counts as competent.

Inhabiting a Social Identity: Attaching to Social Categories

Social identities of any type are inhabited and sustained by regulating behavior to enact with others a repertoire of statuses, i.e., roles. However, far from being fixed or static, roles are dynamic, representing many different forms of statuses associated with a particular identity. For instance, the social identity of teacher might be enacted through such roles as *guide, questioner, evaluator, encourager,* or *director.* Typically, roles, as a form of status, bring certain entitlements for actions, interactions, and ethical ways of relating and being that are associated with the related social identity. Because the specific actions used to enact roles may be marked as beneficial, worthwhile, and valuable by a local community, statuses can position community members advantageously, with privileges to direct or control (i.e., regulate) the behavior of oneself and/or others. To summarize, social identities come to be inhabited agentially and opportunistically by enacting statuses (or roles) that reflect (or are interpreted to reflect) community values and its moral ethos of rights, responsibilities, and duties for engaging in routine activities, which indicates different ways of regulating behaviors.

Identities of competency are commonly valued and desired in all educational arenas whether formal or informal; however, identities of competency are not all the same. On the contrary, the beliefs, values, and practices pertaining to competency will vary from locale to locale and, within any particular community, learners will regulate their engagement in ways that mirror the actions and interactions that represent the local moral ethos toward gaining and displaying competency. For this reason, *identities of competency* must be contextualized to be properly understood.

To enact a situational status (role) associated with competency, learners *attach to* a local social category of competency (Hall, 2004) through stancetaking. Stancetaking is a pervasive communicative activity in which speakers use linguistic resources to evaluate the object of ongoing talk. This evaluation creates and signals a relationship between the speaker and the object of activity. At the same time, it creates an alignment with other interlocutors. Most importantly, stancetaking is observable, public, and interpretable (Du Bois, 2007), highlighting its interactional and relational nature. Put differently, regulating behavior to fill an identity of competency is not a solo act; rather, it involves an interactive, collaborative, and opportunistic process with other social actors, who also evaluate, interpret, and respond to ongoing interactions through stancetaking. The significance of this interactive process is that everyone involved can potentially display recognition or rejection of someone's competency as roles are enacted. In effect, such public recognition through stancetaking makes "the right of ownership" of an identity of competency real for both the individual and the community (Thompson, 2016).

The route to inhabit an identity of competency emerges over interactional time, reproduced across days and months as children (and adults) regulate their behaviors to enact a range of statuses (roles) associated with competency. How stancetaking occurs over interactional time is illustrated by the stance triangle in Figure 4.1. This figure shows how stancetaking is accomplished through a "triplex act" when learners (or mentor/teacher and learners) simultaneously evaluate some focus of concern to align with others in order to attach to a local social category of competency. For example, when an adult mentor responds to a child's question with an evaluation, "whatever you think would work," this evaluation aligns the two speakers (or creates a relationship between them) toward the object of conversation (i.e., how to solve a problem). In learning arenas where the roles of being a thinker, problem solver, or decision maker are marked as competent, such stancetaking activities also align interlocutors with the local social category of competency.

In this example, through stancetaking, the social category of competency (object) is made relevant and locally produced. Attaching oneself and

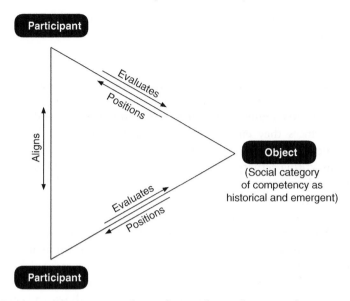

Figure 4.1   The stance triangle: attaching to the social category of competency
(adapted from Du Bois, 2007)

others to this social category is accomplished by utilizing two commonly recognized forms of stances that co-occur in the same utterance: epistemic and affective stances. Epistemic stances in learning settings refer to those instances when a mentor/teacher or child indicates a knowledge-based or authoritative relationship to some object, state of affairs, social category, or other things in the world. For example, when a young child regulates her behavior to announce, "I know! I know how to do that," she is taking an authoritative epistemic stance toward knowing. Similarly, affective stances occur when a mentor/teacher or child indicates an emotion-based relationship to some object, state of affairs, social category, or other things in the world (Ochs, 1996). For example, when a young child offers assistance by smiling and pointing to a display of sound-picture cards and saying "you gotta look at the card," her smile combined with a gesture enacts an affective (or feeling) stance. Both types of stances can be expressed through words and paralinguistic features such as tone of voice, duration, loudness, prosody, gestures, and body positioning. The intriguing aspect of these co-occurring stances is that they are the linguistic resources by which children and adults regulate their behaviors to communicate both cognitive and emotional (feeling and attitudinal) evaluations and states toward actions, objects, and thoughts (Stone & Thompson, 2014). Together these stances create an interpretive frame through which learners enact situational roles to inhabit an identity.

The forms of behavioral regulation used to enact and inhabit identities of competency that we describe here entail a complex process in which learners decide under what circumstances to co-, self-, or other-regulate actions and interactions. Ultimately, it is through behavioral regulation and the stances they enact that learners come to inhabit identities of competency (or any other identity). For example, in an early childhood classroom writing activity, when a child takes up the valued role (status) of help seeker by asking, "uhm:: >how you< spell: ↓wovlfss:" [wolves], they are effectively self-regulating (agentially directing and controlling their behavior to enact an epistemic stance of uncertainty about how to spell wolves). Simultaneously, through prosody and intonation, the child enacts an affective stance that indicates interest in knowing/learning how to spell the word in question. This, in turn, indexes a future state of knowing, when the child will know how to spell "wolves." Meanwhile, a peer sitting nearby self-regulates his own behavior when he responds with an epistemic stance of certainty: "I can sp↑ell: >I:↑know< I know." Through the combined use of the modal verb "can" and the cognitive verb "to know," the child's response expresses ability (competency). Likewise, placing emphasis on the pronoun "I" and the verb "know" suggests a positive attitude toward knowing. What this brief interaction illustrates is how, by regulating their behaviors, these children are using stances to index and attach to the local social category of competency. In collaboration with one another, they effectively enact roles to inhabit an implicit identity of competency.

The meaning of these collaborative stancetaking actions emerges in the context of social interaction because people use stances to create interpretive frames for the roles they enact (cf. Thompson & Dori-Hacohen, 2012). Yet the interactional context of stancetaking is inherently interrelated with its larger sociocultural context, in this case, a classroom in which specific learning processes are marked as competent (e.g., asking others for help, displaying one's understanding of a construct, assisting others, etc.). Therefore, when individuals utilize stancetaking as an interpretive frame, that is, a sense-making resource, their utterances are bridging two levels of context. The first of these two levels is the dialogic context of meaning-making, that is, the interactional construction of context through the co-construction of meaning. The second is the historically built context of the local community – for example, classrooms or after-school clubs. Each of these levels of context is always in play as interlocutors regulate their stancetaking actions to inhabit identities. What is more, because of the inherent connections between the dialogic and the community levels, the behaviors that participants use to inhabit their identities of competency end up reflecting the values and moral ethos of their learning arena.

Inhabiting an Identity of Competency: Formal and Informal Learning Arenas

To illustrate the ways that children actively regulate their behaviors to inhabit identities of competency, we present data taken from two year-long video ethnographies of teaching and learning in two unique urban settings: a first-grade classroom and an after-school program involving second through sixth graders and their undergraduate mentors. These settings not only illuminate different local definitions of competency but also show how such definitions influence the roles and stances that participants enact in order to inhabit identities of competency within their community.

A Formal Learning Arena: Ms. Winter's Classroom

The first learning setting is a first-grade classroom in an urban, northern California school with children from diverse linguistic and ethnic backgrounds. In this classroom, the teacher, Ms. Winter, utilizes instructional practices that position children as having the right and responsibility to self-, co-, and other-regulate engagement in literacy learning. To this end, she has repeatedly marked four particular roles for engagement as important for displaying and gaining competency: help seeker, help giver, evaluator of knowledge (metacognitive acts), and tool user (in this case, the use of sound-spelling cards). These roles defined the community ethos for enacting competency and constituted important components of the social category of competency. Not surprisingly, the children consistently used these roles to regulate their own and each other's engagement in literacy learning (Stone & Hart, 2007).

Excerpt 4.1 illustrates how children, without the benefit of knowing the "correct" response, used the emergent social category of competency to regulate their behaviors. That is, they enacted roles associated with being a competent literacy learner as a proleptic (future in the making) sign system to inhabit an identity of competency. This excerpt is taken from a writing lesson where Ms. Winter has shared a recipe for grilled cheese sandwiches and coached children in basic cooking vocabulary. The

Excerpt 4.1 *Enacting competency: "how ta spell sauce?"*

Alexi	*((Looking at his paper and engaged in private speech.))*	4.10
	sau::ce.	4.11
	s::aw::	4.12
	how ta spell sa::uce?	4.13
	((quiet voice))	4.14
Alberto	*((Moves toward Alexi looking at his paper.))*	4.15
	hunh?	4.16
Alexi	saw:se:	4.17
Alberto	S uh: O	4.18
	((In an effort to help, says each letter aloud.))	4.19
Alexi	*((Looking down at his paper and writing.))*	4.20
	S-O *((Saying each letter aloud in private speech.))*	4.21
Alberto	s::: au:	4.22
	I <u>mean</u> capital O	4.23
	s::: au::	4.24
	((Stands up and moves next to Alexi, then looks down at	4.25
	Alexi's paper.))	4.26
	look at the sound card and say the <u>sound</u>.	4.27
	s:au::ce. ᵒlook at the <u>sauce</u>.ᵒ	4.28
Alexi	s:au::ce *((Private speech while focusing on his writing.))*	4.29
	>how spell sau<u>ce</u>?<	4.30
	s :au :ce	4.31
	s ::	4.32
Brandon	sau:ce ? I don't know	4.33
Alexi	>I do.<	4.34
	do::ne.	4.35
	>see (.) I done<	4.36

children were asked to think about their favorite food, write a recipe for it, and draw an accompanying illustration. Two of the focal children in this study, Alexi and Alberto, sit together at a table with a third child, Brandon. Alexi has decided to write a recipe for a ham sandwich with "green sauce."

In this excerpt, Alexi self-regulates his behavior to spell "sauce" by using private speech (lines 4.10–4.14). His use of private speech is an indicator of competency because Ms. Winter often marked this form of engagement as a desired method for solving spelling problems during writing activities (see Stone & Hart, 2007). When his attempt fails, he asks Alberto for help ("how ta spell sauce?"), thereby enacting the status of help seeker, which is another indicator of competency in this setting. Here, "how ta spell sauce?" is an epistemic stance of certainty toward meta knowledge, that is, knowing how and when to evaluate the quality of one's knowledge. Although Alexi did not know how to spell the word "sauce," he *knew* a strategy for competently seeking out that information (ask a classmate for help). Through these actions, Alexi enacts the locally marked and valued status of help seeker and evaluator of knowledge through metacognition (or thinking about thinking). Through stancetaking, Alexi is both indexing and attaching to the local social category of competency as he vies to fill the identity of a competent literacy learner.

Alberto, on hearing Alexi's question, aligns and collaborates with him by regulating his own behavior to take on the status of help giver. In this role, Alberto enacts an epistemic stance of knowledgeability by moving closer to Alexi and beginning to spell "sauce" out loud (lines 4.15, 4.18–4.19). Alexi co-regulates his behavior to collaborate by beginning to write each of the letters that he hears, which also counts as displaying an epistemic stance of knowledgeability (lines 4.20–4.21). As Alexi writes, Alberto continues to enact his status of help giver by figuring out how to spell "sauce" and moving to stand next to Alexi for a better view of his paper. Next, Alberto attempts to other-regulate Alexi's attention toward a solution strategy, telling him "look at the sound card and say the <u>sound</u>" (line 4.27). Besides enacting an epistemic stance of certainty, these utterances convey information designed to regulate behavior and, taken together, they align Alberto with the local category of competency.

Although he does not reply explicitly, Alexi self-regulates with epistemic stances in private speech to quickly reevaluate his knowledge (a metacognitive act), ">I do.< done. see I done<" (lines 4.34–4.36). Here again, Alexi's action reenacts a locally marked status role of evaluator of knowledge. Through stancetaking in these roles, Alexi indexes and attaches to the local social category of competency as he works to fill the identity of a competent literacy learner.

So far, we have illustrated how children in a first-grade classroom regulated their behavior and utilized valued behaviors as a means to inhabit identities of competency. Here, the indicators of competency (help seeking, help giving, evaluating knowledge, knowing how to use tools/strategies) became part of the locally shared category of competency. Furthermore, they were interpreted and used by children to enact roles by self-, co-, and other-regulating behaviors. In assuming these roles, the children took stances to attach themselves to their community's social category of competency. As each child negotiated and enacted the statuses (roles) deemed important and advantageous for competent engagement, they were showing competency in the present, even though they did not yet have fully developed understandings of how to spell or read particular words or passages of text. In other words, vying to inhabit identities of competency functioned as a proleptic sign system of competency that mediated their regulatory processes in literacy learning.

Although these children experienced a unique learning arena where the teacher shared learning goals with her students by creating open-ended literacy tasks, they still expected the teacher, Ms. Winter, to be the director of their learning goals and the ultimate evaluator of their progress. The next example, taken from an informal setting, shows a different but complementary approach to academic learning where the children are expected to create, plan, execute, and evaluate their activities. This informal approach to learning changes the social category of competency and the available resources, i.e., statuses/roles, for inhabiting identities of competency, all of which influences the ways learners engage in a system of regulatory processes.

An Informal Learning Arena: The Magical Web in the 5th Dimension

The next setting that we introduce is a unique after-school program referred to as the Magical Web in the 5th Dimension, referred to by its members simply as "The Web." The site's playful approach reflects its purpose, namely to reframe academic learning through the lens of discovery and play. The Web involved a collaboration between a university and a local elementary school. As part of this collaboration, undergraduates took an on-site course in cultural-historical theories of psychological development, in which they were also trained in how to mentor children in project-based learning environments. With this training, the undergraduates, referred to as Wizard's Assistants, or WAs for short, mentored children in projects, as guided by open-ended, collaborative activity guides. These guides offered children avenues of exploration rather than explicitly detailing specific steps or end goals for a project. In general, the guides' directions required children to (1) select or create a project that interested them, (2) create a plan of action, (3) present their plan (prospectus) to the larger "Web" community, (4) carry out their plan, and (5) share their completed projects with family and friends at biyearly gatherings.

In the context of The Web, the practical methods of engagement that were marked as important, beneficial, and desirable tended to be those that encouraged children to be collaborative agents in generating the focus of their project; to research what needed to be known by utilizing books, the Internet, and other resources like friends and family; to plan what needed to be done; and, finally, to implement their plans, making necessary adjustments along the way.

Over time, The Web community's values and expectations vis-à-vis learning and engagement led to unique and noteworthy circumstances. For example, participating children took on responsibility for constructing their own open-ended "activity guides" by simplifying the task to "plan, share, and do." This abbreviation removed the necessity of a physically written document and resulted in children not only defining the goal-directed activity but also taking on central responsibility for its completion. This, in turn, resulted in a social category of competency that varied from most formal learning arenas where teachers (and other adults) typically define and initiate goal-directed activities and also take on primary responsibility for evaluating what is known and what needs to be known. In contrast, within The Web, the regulatory processes of both the children and their adult mentors led to interesting differences in the meaning of the roles/statuses that children used to inhabit identities of competency.

To illustrate the roles (and the linguistic stances) that were used to attach to the social category of competency in The Web, we draw data from an organic gardening project. This project involved four children who called themselves "Extreme Gardeners" – Mimi, a second grader; Koby, a third grader; Paige, a fourth grader; and Jake, a fifth grader – and Bella, a WA. Bella, an undergraduate in her senior year, had already taken three university courses in cultural-historical theories of psychological development, one of which was held on-site. From these courses, she had developed an understanding of the role of a mentor as a participant who guides and collaborates to support learning as an active involvement process. For her, the practical actions of this involvement (i.e., the roles she enacted) tended to involve co-regulation with the goal of assisting children in both co- and self-regulation, the overarching aim of which was to support the children in achieving their own goals.

To inhabit the social identity of mentor, Bella's most commonly enacted roles were clarifier (information seeker) and observer/encourager. In her role as clarifier, she consistently used memory and clarification questions to coach children in drawing on prior knowledge for productive engagement in problem-solving. In the role of encourager/observer, Bella vocalized positive observations about the children's progress and their creative solutions to problems. She also shared noticings about plan progressions to help the children evaluate their progress. Through these roles, Bella marked helping, listening, thinking, and collective remembering as competent ways of engaging collaboratively.

The children's understandings about competent engagement tended to mirror Bella's. There were, however, some variations. For example, in interview data, the children defined thinking as being "flexible with ideas," "figuring out what to do with others," and "sharing ideas." They defined collaboration as "listening," "staying on task," and "sharing," for example "we all share things" (e.g., tools, supplies, ideas, etc.). In terms of helping, the children's definition was similar to Bella's in that it involved asking for and giving help; however, it also included "taking a vote to solve a problem" and "helping others with problems." Over time, the constituents of the social category of competency included both Bella's ideas and the interpretation and elaboration of these ideas by the children.

We now turn to an illustration of how children in the garden project attached themselves and others to the social category of competency through stancetaking during the enactment of roles. The interaction in Excerpt 4.2 took place after the children had read about soil percolation and how to test for it: (1) dig a hole 15 centimeters wide and 30 centimeters deep (1 foot); (2) fill the hole with water; and (3) time how long it takes for the water to be absorbed by the soil. Regarding the measurement of the holes, the children (who were missing their rulers) had already come up with the idea of using inch markings indicated on their trowels. Reasoning that the exact conversion of 2.54 centimeters to 1 inch was not necessary, and that the 3 to 1 ratio was easier to remember, they had determined to use the heuristic of 3 centimeters to 1 inch for measuring hole size.

This excerpt begins with Bella (WA-B) standing next to a garden plot with her foot on the edge looking down toward the children as they are digging holes to test for percolation. In her role as observer, Bella evaluates Mimi's hole as being "↑almost do↑ne::" with a combined epistemic stance of certainty about knowing and an affective stance displaying interest (line 4.37). In response, Mimi also uses an epistemic stance of certainty about knowing as she clarifies what she is doing, "I'm wi::dening my hole," a stance that indexes the local category of competency, which includes "staying on task" and evaluating progress. Here, Mimi uses an affective stance through prosody to engage in a *polite* clarification that also accomplishes a brief evaluation of working toward her goals – a wider hole. Through these actions, Mimi is co-regulating her behavior with Bella to take on the competent status of evaluator. Although Mimi is being polite, she does not orient to Bella but rather continues to look down and work on widening her hole. This is a pattern of orienting toward the "task"; as a marker of competency, it is seen among all the children throughout this excerpt, as well as across this and other activities.

Excerpt 4.2 *Enacting competency: negotiation and collaboration*

WA-B:	Mimi you↑'re:: ↑almost do↓ne::	4.37
	((*Looking down at Mimi digging her hole.*))	4.38
Mimi:	I'm ↑wi::dening my ho:le	4.39
	((*Continuing to look down as she works on digging.*))	4.40
Jake:	this ↑hole is [un abyss:: ((*Digging, looking down.*))	4.41
WA-B:	[remember your hole should be:: >↑how wide<	4.42
	((*Looking down at the children.*))	4.43
Paige:	my ho::le got ↑small:::er ((*Looking down and digging.*))	4.44
WA-B:	how ↑big should the hole be guy°s::°	4.45
Koby:	one fuht ((*Looking down and digging.*))	4.46
Mimi:	uh foo::t ((*Looking down and digging.*))	4.47
Koby:	>no< fif↑teen:: (.) >centi<meters ((*Looking down, digging.*))	4.48
WA-B:	how wi::- o uh how much is 15 >centimeters< in inches	4.49
Paige:	[five inches ((*Looking down and digging.*))	4.50
Koby	[(unclear)	4.51
Jake:	three inches ((*Looking down and digging.*))	4.52
WA-B:	th↑ree:: inches↑	4.53
Paige:	five ((*Looking down and digging.*))	4.54
Koby:	>yeah five< ((*Looking down and digging.*))	4.55
WA-B:	how'd ja get—fi:ve Paige↓	4.56
Paige:	um:: because. five ti:- times three equals fifteen and.	4.57
	we know that three would be too small *so* ((*Looking down and*	4.58
	digging.))	4.59
WA-B:	what's what's the three representing↓ in your five times three↑	4.60
Koby:	↑in:ches ((*Looking down and digging.*))	4.61
Jake:	↑I'm:: making up fi::ve feet ((*Looking down, digging.*))	4.62
WA-B:	how many centi>meters< are in an inch (.) guys↑	4.63
Mimi:	three:: ((*Looking down and digging.*))	4.64
WA-B:	three:: (.) so:: if I want >↑fif<teen: centimeters how many	4.65
	inches↑	4.66
Jake:	four ((*Looking down and digging.*))	4.67
Mimi:	three:: six [nine twelve. fifteen ((*Counting out loud to herself*	4.68
	and digging.))	4.69
WA-B:	[four times three↑	4.70
Jake:	four times three is twelve ((*Looking down and digging.*))	4.71
WA-B:	we want fifteen inches↑ so how many in- centimeters so	4.72
	how many inches (.) is that↑	4.73
Jake:	actually y↑eah that is five inches ((*Looking down, digging.*))	4.74
WA-B:	>five inches<	4.75
Koby:	yeah five inches ((*Looking down and digging.*))	4.76

Mimi's behavior contrasts with what is typically observed in formal learning settings, where children orient themselves toward a teacher, who is ultimately responsible for directing, controlling, and evaluating engagement. In The Web, however, competency involves self-regulating behavior to "stay on task" and to "evaluate" one's thinking/knowledge. Both of these are a means of collaborating with the group in that evaluations and monitoring on task behavior are accomplished with others through co-regulation toward the object of activity. For these reasons, Mimi's own evaluative response (line 4.39) is a clarification that aligns with Bella to attach to The Web's socially shared category of competency. To emphasize this point, here in this community, epistemic authority for evaluating, thinking, and collaborating is placed in the hands of the children. Children take on this form of authority, an epistemic position, as they regulate their behavior to inhabit an identity of competency in this local context.

Yet Bella's explicit identity as an adult WA also brings with it an epistemic position of authority. Bella is older than the children, more experienced, and also a university student. Nevertheless, the statuses that she chooses to enact vary from those of instructors in formal learning settings. In The Web, children are expected to self- and co-regulate their behaviors to control, direct, and evaluate their own engagement. As a consequence, Bella's evaluations, questions, and noticings are not intended to define or direct children's goals but rather to assist them in regulating their behaviors such that they can achieve their goals. Bella enacts different roles to help organize the activity as agential so that children can actively regulate their behaviors to reflect, remember, and control what is said and what is done for pragmatic actions and knowledge construction. In other words, Bella draws from the historically built, shared assumptions of The Web community to interpret her epistemic position as one of assisting children in becoming intellectual agents of goal-directed activity through concomitant collaborative learning processes (e.g., collective remembering and reflections on and evaluations of thinking or metacognition).

Bella's interpretations of mentorship are captured in the questions she directs to the children. She begins this questioning with "remember your hole should be:: >how ↑wide<" (line 4.42), which she slightly reformulates moments later (line 4.45). Here, she takes an epistemic stance of certainty to enact (construct) her authority. However, this authority (epistemic position) is to assist children in shared metacognition, i.e., collaborative remembering, so that they can pursue their goal. Indeed, as the children collaborate with Bella, they do co-regulate their behavior to think together.

This collaborative thinking occurs as Koby says "one fuht" and Mimi repeats his response with a clearer enunciation of "foot" (line 4.46). Koby follows this repetition with a self-repair, ">no< fif↑teen:: (.) >centi<meters." This interaction occurs as the children continue working together, digging and looking down at the hole, rather than gesturally aligning with Bella. The children's utterances and gestures enact collaborative epistemic stances of certainty about knowing, even when they self-correct. Accomplished in collaboration with Bella, their stances work to attach them to the local category of competency as they vie to fill an identity of competency.

The next part of this sequence begins with another question posed by Bella, who requests a clarification of the conversion of 15 centimeters to inches (line 4.49). Similar to the prior exchange, this question of Bella's initiates collective remembering by the children. It also leads to a noncontested response in which 15 centimeters is converted to 5 inches, reflecting the children's earlier heuristic of 3 centimeters to 1 inch. This interaction once again allows the children to enact the role of "thinker" (i.e., figuring out what to do collaboratively). And, as they co-regulate their behavior to remember and think together, they use stancetaking to attach to the social category of competency, with Bella's question acting as a catalyst for this process.

The final sequence of utterances is initiated when Bella begins to ask clarifying questions about the children's conversion of centimeters to inches. Through these questions, Bella inhabits the explicit but locally defined social identity of mentor by taking up the role of clarifier. Here, she uses epistemic stances of certainty about wanting to know what the three represents in "five times three," how many centimeters are in an inch, and how many inches are in 15 centimeters. Although these same questions might occur in classroom settings, in the context of The Web, they have a different function. Here, these questions are not used to direct activity implicitly but rather to assist children in remembering those understandings (competencies) that have been marked as important, beneficial, and desirable for accomplishing their collaborative goals. In other words, these children view Bella as assisting them, not assessing them. For this reason, she is a co-participant rather than a director of activity. This relationship explains why these children do not feel that she holds the same epistemic position as a teacher.

Not surprisingly, Bella's questions elicit forms of collaboration as she helps the children remember information that they had investigated and agreed on earlier. For example, Mimi regulates her behavior to engage in reflective thought by quietly counting in threes to herself (private speech) but just loud enough for others to hear. This is an implicit form of collaboration because others have access to her thinking as she figures out how many inches are in 15 centimeters (lines 4.68–4.69). In this reflection, Mimi is both enacting a collaborative "thinker" status and using epistemic stances of certainty as she counts. With these actions, Mimi indexes and attaches to the local category of competency. Jake and Koby use epistemic stances of certainty to agree that 15 centimeters is 5 inches (lines 4.71, 4.74, 4.76). In their interaction, they co-regulate their behavior to collaborate by "staying on task," "listening" to each other, and remembering. In doing so, they also enact valued roles and use epistemic and affective stances to index and attach to the social category of competency, thus inhabiting a local identity of competency.

To summarize, by enacting status roles to meet situational demands, children regulate their behavior to utilize multimodal forms of stancetaking, which allows them to inhabit implicit identities of competency as an embodied and dialogic identity in practice. Through this learning practice, children interactively regulated their behaviors to evaluate and align themselves and others to attach to the local social category of competency. In this way, identity and competency became linked through a process of semiotic mediation where the collaborative construction and use of signs (local indicators of competency) became a constitutive part of their identities of competency.

Reimagining competency as an emergent and implicit social identity situated in learning areas offers a unique way of viewing competency not solely as an individual's ability or knowledge base but as a relational process – the relational ways of doing, being, and knowing with social others that foster both individual and collective competencies. Observing the relational processes of vying to inhabit an identity of competency makes it possible for research practitioners, educators, and students to "see" how learners utilize contextual resources to regulate their psychological and pragmatic behaviors to initiate, direct, and sustain engagement during ambiguities and complexities of learning activities. By observing this process, we can better understand not only how learners participate in the co-construction of competency but also how they become an authoritative initiator of the activity – that is, the author of one's own learning, utilizing different forms of behavioral regulation.

CHAPTER 5

Contextual Mood and Regulatory Processes

Both the calm and the flurried moments of learning contexts are permeated by moods that influence the ways learners regulate their engagement. Moods in these learning contexts can range from the lightheartedness of pretend play activities to the frustration and stress of test-taking. No matter what the mood is, they saturate learning situations and influence how children control and direct their behavior. Yet we are just beginning to understand the role of emotions in learning activities and how they mediate the ways in which learners regulate their engagement. The reason for our limited understanding is due, in large part, to the theoretical assumptions of psychological approaches that consider emotions, including moods, to be states internal to the individual (Scherer, 2000). This focus leads to what Sawyer (2005) calls *methodological individualism* in which understandings about emotions are derived from individuals' retrospective thinking and descriptions of their feelings. These self-reports about emotions are not designed to take into account either the flow of emergent feelings in social contexts or how these feelings influence learners' regulatory processes.

At present, there is a sea change in how emotions are being conceptualized. Individualistic views are gradually receding in favor of relational perspectives in which emotions (referred to as "feelings" or "affect" here) are seen as emerging from social processes, i.e., through interactions with others (Sabin, 2014). This change is reflected in educational research studies aimed at capturing how emotions are an inherent part of the social and interactional processes of learning contexts (Do & Schallert, 2004; Meyer & Turner, 2006). Inspired by a need for a more socialized and relational conception of "emotion," researchers are figuring out better methodologies to grasp the relationship of the individual to their social situations. This chapter contributes to these new understandings of the role of emotions in learning practices by offering a unique way of conceptualizing the interrelationship between feelings and context through the idea of a *contextual mood*. Here, in contrast to individualistic notions, mood is defined as emerging from socially distributed, interactive mechanisms, which, in turn, create and sustain moods in the lived experiences of learning. Our conceptualization of contextual moods foregrounds their important role in shaping how learners regulate their engagement in routine activities of learning.

To show how contextual moods emerge and influence learners' regulatory processes of thinking and doing, we will first draw from sociocultural theory to explain our approach to emotions. Next, we will describe the concept of stancetaking to show how this linguistic resource is used in talk to create and communicate feelings over interactional time. We follow this description with an explanation of how feelings emerge through stancetaking to create a contextual mood. To illustrate the emergence of a contextual mood, we will present data showing how a contextual mood for collaborative problem-solving develops, soliciting particular forms of behavioral regulation during literacy learning. Finally, following Vygotsky's (1935) claim that the "dynamic and relative interpretation of environment is the most important source of information for paedology" (p. 346), we will close this chapter by arguing that the dynamic and relative interpretation of classroom mood is a crucial source for understanding regulatory processes in learning contexts.

Our approach to mood is grounded in sociocultural theories of human learning and development and follows a generally Vygotskian frame in thinking about the dialectical relationship between the individual and the collective. In particular, we develop two key concepts about emotion found in Vygotsky's writings: emotional experience (perezhivanie) and the socially contingent nature of emotions.

First, Vygotsky (1934/1986) argues that affective processes permeate thought and actions. In effect, he is pointing to the importance of emotional experience in how learners decide to regulate their engagement in learning activities. As Vygotsky (1935) contends, "The emotional experience [perezhivanie] arising from any situation or from any aspect of his environment, determines what kind of influence this situation or this environment will have on the child" (pp. 339–340). With this quote, Vygotsky is proposing that the situated emotional experiences of the child organize the system of regulatory behaviors engaged in by learners. When considered in light of learning interactions, as we will do in this chapter, Vygotsky's insight suggests that, if we wish to understand the impact of social interactions on the regulatory processes of learners, then we need to understand emotional experience in the ever-changing emergence and complexities of learning contexts.

Second, although Vygotsky's key concept for characterizing emotion, perezhivanie, is typically understood as referring to the emotional experience of the individual, we feel that adding a concern with the socially emergent concept of mood is fully consistent with Vygotsky's approach to emotions. Indeed, Vygotsky points to the socially contingent nature of emotion in his discussion of art. In *The Psychology of Art*, Vygotsky (1971) writes,

> Art is the social technique of emotion, a tool of society which brings the most intimate and personal aspects of our being into the circle of social life. It would be more correct to say that emotion becomes personal when every one of us experiences a work of art; it becomes personal without ceasing to be social. (p. 249)

In this quote, Vygotsky is specifically arguing that the creation of art functions as a visual and material cultural tool or sign that we create to foster emotional experiences. In effect, he is claiming semiotic (tool and sign) mediation is an inherent part of emotional experiences. Of significance, these mediational processes represent the unification of the social and individual and through this unification affect and thought are woven together. In fact, in Vygotsky's (1978) own words, "behind every thought there is an affective-volitional tendency" (p. 150). This claim means that the social construction of meaning and thought with others is first saturated with feelings and motivational (or directive) tendencies. Thus, extending Vygotsky's thinking on experiencing the influence of the "environment" and of art to the area of emotion requires a more socialized conception of "emotion," one that better conceptualizes the relationship between the individual and the emotional aspects inherent in our construction of social situations. Consequently, in this chapter, we propose the concept of contextual mood as an analytical tool for grasping how the social-emotional whole of our ways of being in cultural activities comes to be a constitutive part of the situated regulatory system utilized by individuals to engage in learning. We also suggest that, like art, mood "becomes personal without ceasing to be social" and we propose that this socialized notion of mood offers a productive way of better understanding the role of emotion in the regulatory processes of thinking and doing in learning contexts.

Utilizing a Vygotskyian approach, we characterize mood in holistic terms and provide a conception of mood that is distributed across time and space. In this sense, mood does not characterize an individual but rather a setting or a context. This conception draws on an everyday usage of mood, as in "There was a somber mood in the stadium after the home team lost the game," or "The mood of the classroom lightened when the teacher announced that the final exam would be open book." Here, "mood" is not so much the property of an individual but of a particular setting, in which it is distributed across people. Further, mood is not a temporally punctuated event; instead, it must be developed and sustained across time.

Our conception of mood as being distributed across time and space goes against the largely synchronic (points in time) approach taken by emotion researchers, who generally view emotions as relatively punctuated events. From their more traditional perspective, there is no need to string together moments in time in order to understand emotions. In fact, when time is taken into consideration, it is employed merely as a way of differentiating between different discrete emotions (e.g., anger, happiness, fear). In this approach, any given emotion might as well be considered as a point in time rather than as a trajectory across multiple points in time; in other words, time is not essential to emotion (e.g., Harmon-Jones, Bastian, & Harmon-Jones, 2016). The timeless emotion view is reinforced by self-report methods that measure feelings in isolated moments, without attending to what happens across time. Thus, this view takes emotion as something that effectively exists "out of time." In contrast to this synchronic approach, we employ a diachronic (across time) construct of mood. In our view, in fact, time is essential because moods can be enduring, not just fleeting[1]. If we wish to understand mood, then we must attend to mood in time.

Furthermore, because moods can be experienced by a collective (not just individuals), they must come into existence through social interactions. That is, moods have to arise through some type of back-and-forth activity between people and across time. Here, too, we differ from traditional emotion researchers, who typically locate emotion within individuals. In contrast, we locate mood in the interactional context. Theoretical and empirical work in linguistic anthropology and micro sociology (Atkinson & Heritage, 1984; Duranti & Goodwin, 1992; Goffman, 1974) has illuminated how context is an emergent phenomenon arising from back-and-forth communicative processes. Interlocutors within a social scene draw on background information about their setting, what social positions (statuses) and actions are appropriate within it, and what historically built shared assumptions are there in play. Simultaneously, interlocutors'

---

[1] Applying the notion of timescales (Lemke, 2000), we find that stances are short phenomena – on the order of seconds – and more individual in nature. (Although stances are socially distributed phenomena, they typically refer back to the speaker.) In contrast, mood is a longer phenomenon – on the order of minutes and, perhaps, even hours – that is distributed across time and space.

activities act back on the communicative context, further shaping it. In this way, context is always emergent and dynamically produced: individuals contribute to the definition of the local context and the local context contributes to the definitions of the individuals (Thompson & Dori-Hacohen, 2012, Heritage, 1984; see also Cole, 1995, for a discussion of the mutually constitutive nature of context and event).

As we are emphasizing here, moods are built from the communicative acts of individual persons; however, moods are always more than the sum of the individuals' parts (qua emotional states). The emotional states of individual participants are, of course, important for understanding mood; nevertheless, understanding mood necessarily involves going beyond any one individual's emotional experience or even a simple addition of the emotional experiences of participants. It is the bidirectional relationship between the situation of development and the development of the situation that the mood is created. This dual developmental (aka "genetic") aspect of the production of mood means that mood has a temporal dimension. Furthermore, we see mood as spatially emergent and distributed across persons in a setting as they regulate their engagement in activity. Thus, attending to mood necessarily requires an understanding of the emergent distribution of "mood" within that space. In sum, understanding mood requires a rich understanding of that which exists between and beyond participants. Similarly, regulatory processes, as influenced by contextual mood(s), must also be accounted for as relational phenomena that emerge from the creation of learning contexts.

Stancetaking and Mood

The very qualities of mood that make it an interesting way to study the interrelationships between contexts and feelings, including its socially and temporally distributed nature, have made it difficult to study until now. Mood is often described as "intractable" and thought to be "untranscribable" in both everyday and scientific discourse (see Throop, 2014). Here, we offer a unique approach for making moods "transcribable" by utilizing the linguistic anthropological concept of stance. In talk, stances are linguistic resources used to signal and create an evaluation of and alignment with ongoing talk by communicating feelings and thoughts. Specifically, they are the methods (linguistic and other) by which individuals regulate their behaviors to display, communicate, and interactively produce "a socially recognized point of view" on experience and action with others (Ochs, 1993, p. 288).

Every utterance both enacts a stance and emerges from dialogic inter-action (Jaffe, 2009; Kärkkäinen, 2004; Ochs, 1990). In the linguistic sense, stance involves a "triplex act" of evaluation in which an individual speaker simultaneously (1) evaluates some focus of concern and (2) positions themselves in relation to that focus while also (3) aligning themselves with other participants over interactional time (Du Bois, 2007; see also Chapter 4 for an in-depth explanation of stancetaking). Thus, stancetaking is a fundamentally relational form of social action and is intersubjective in the sense that it always indicates a relation between a speaking subject and an interlocutor (Kärkkäinen, 2003). Further, stances are culturally and historically linked to local communicative processes of stancetaking and the recognizability of any stance is dependent on and "shaped by culture and custom" (Precht, 2003, p. 240; see also Ochs, 1996). Stance researchers have demonstrated that stance is an interactional achievement; however, we wish to emphasize here that, for speakers, stance operates as an indication of something about the speaking subject. In other words, although stancetaking is not an individual act, stance indicates the speaking subject's relationship to some object, event, person, or state of affairs. As such, stance is understood by interactional participants to indicate something about an individual in a dialogic context.

In this chapter, we describe two general types of stances: epistemic and affective (Ochs, 1996). When considered in classroom interactions, epis-temic stance refers to those instances of talk when the teacher or the child indicates a knowledge-based relationship to some object, state of affairs, or other thing in the world (Ochs, 1996). Similarly, affective stance refers to those instances of talk in which the teacher or child indicates an emotion-based relationship to some object, state of affairs, or thing in the world (Goodwin, 2007). We employ a distinction between epistemic and affec-tive stances as a productive analytic. By so doing, we do not intend to suggest that this is a distinction that inheres in the phenomena in the world, or that knowledge and emotion exist as separate phenomena in the world. Rather, our point is simply that every utterance has elements of both epistemic and affective stances.

Epistemic and affective stances, which may co-occur in the same utter-ance (Schieffelin, 1996), can be indicated directly by the denotational content of words – for example, "I hate tests" – or indirectly by the indexical content of the forms used – for example, "Making us take these tests is a form of torture." Further, stances are not limited to the expression of words but may also be indexically indicated through tone of voice, duration, loudness, prosody, gestures, body positioning, and other paralinguistic features such as pitch or tempo (see Biber & Finegan, 1989; Goodwin, 2007). For example, in a writing activity, when a child asks, "Uhm:: how you spell: ↓wovlfss:" and a peer responds, "I can sp↑ell:: I: ↑know:: I know," an epistemic stance is being made in multiple ways. At the referential level, the peer is claiming an epistemic stance through the combined use of the modal verb "can" and the cognitive verb "to know" to express ability. Further, this child is simultaneously taking an affective stance by placing emphasis on the pronoun "I" and the verb "know," thereby suggesting a positive attitude toward that knowing. Importantly, these same words could, in different contexts, indicate different stances, just as different words in similar contexts could indicate the same stances. For this reason, the communicative resources used to signal a stance must be understood in context to fully determine their function. By extension, understanding mood requires understanding the context of the interaction as it unfolds.

Emergence of a Contextual Mood

When learners and teachers or peers control and direct (i.e., self-regulate) their use of stances, they are using linguistic resources to achieve interactional goals with others. In this process, contextual moods emerge from the interaction of stances of people viewed across time. Accordingly, stancetaking provides a way of characterizing some of the elements that contribute to the emergence of a mood through regulatory processes. The creation of mood via stance, however, is not a simple matter of adding up all the stances to get the mood. Rather, it is much more like a chemical combination in which the properties of the resulting molecule are significantly different from the properties of the elements on their own (Vygotsky, 1987). It is in the complex combinatorics of stance that a contextual mood emerges.

To illustrate how a contextual mood emerges from stancetaking over interactional time, and how it solicits particular forms of behavioral regulation, we present five contiguously occurring excerpts drawn from a reading lesson in a first-grade classroom located in an urban school in northern California. In this event, a young learner, Andy, is asked to identify which three letters produce the "ch" phoneme at the end of a word. Andy and his classmates are expected to know from prior instruction that the /*ch*/ phoneme is spelled "ch" at the beginning of a word and "tch" at the end. The children are also expected to use the sound-spelling picture cards displayed on a back wall as visual tools to help them remember the correct spelling.

Emergent Mood and the Regulation of Attention

This instructional event begins in Excerpt 5.1 as Ms. Winter writes the word "fetch" incorrectly ("fech") on a whiteboard and asks the children to evaluate the spelling. (Note that in the transcriptions that follow, capital letters indicate that participants are saying letters aloud; phonemes placed between slashes indicate that participants are saying the sounds of letters aloud.)

In the interaction in Excerpt 5.1, Ms. Winter says the word "fetch" out loud and uses clearly viewable mouthing gestures and emphatic stress to mark each phoneme in this vocabulary word (line 5.11). Her communicative markings enact both epistemic and affective linguistic stances. First, Ms.

Excerpt 5.1 *"does this say fetch?"*

Ms. Winter:	((*Looking at students sitting on rug in front of her.*))	5.10
	fe::>tch:< ((*Dramatically enunciating the digraph /ch/.*))	5.11
	((*Quickly looks down at the whiteboard, begins	5.12
	to write "fe[ch" instead of "fetch".*))	5.13
Brontie:	[°bird fe:tch° ((*Whispering.*))	5.14
Students:	((*Slightly leaning in and attentively looking up at Ms. Winter	5.15
	as she writes.*))	5.16
Ms. Winter:	((*Still writing the word looking at the whiteboard	5.17
	does: this say↓:: fet↑::[ch ((*Slight melodic quality, evenly	5.18
	metered rhythm.*))	5.19
	[((*Looks to the children and runs	5.20
	finger under "fech" on white board.*))*.*))	5.21
Students:	[(((*Gazing between teacher and written word."*))	5.22
	[n::o[::	5.23
Ms. Winter:	[>y↑::es ↑it do:es <- fe:tch: = ((*Stronger melodic	5.24
	prosody.*))	5.25
	((*Pointing to the board, looks to the word quickly, then runs	5.26
	her finger underneath the word.*))	5.27
	=[>but is that the ↑right way to spell ↑it< ((*Shifts into	5.28
	slightly lower tone; directive tone/quality.*))	5.29
	[(((*Looks up at the class.*))	5.30
Students:	↑no:: :[: ((*Choral response, emphatic lengthened and	5.31
	loud, with some children indicating "no"	5.32
	with side-to-side head movements .*))	5.33
Ms. Winter:	[no:::=	5.34
	[(((*Lifts up board for class to see, then looks at it.*))	5.35
Serge:	[>no<	5.36
	[(((*Lifts his shoulders and head up as he raises his	5.37
	hand and shakes it in the air.*))	5.38

Winter's emphatic stress of each phoneme indexes an epistemic stance of importance. Her gestural and verbal emphases simultaneously enact an affective stance of seriousness that accomplishes an implicit directive for children to pay close attention to the sounds of the word being written on the whiteboard. In this way, Ms. Winter's affective stance discloses her attitude toward the activity, while also cuing the children to appropriate regulatory actions for engagement in the activity. These stancetaking actions contribute to an emerging mood of collaborative problem-solving; further-more, this contextual mood is becoming intertwined with locally desired ways to control and direct behavior during problem-solving.

The children regulate their behavior to co-participate in Ms. Winter's stances by slightly leaning toward her and looking up attentively at the whiteboard as she writes (lines 5.15–5.16). Through these regulatory actions, the students index both their epistemic stances of attentiveness and their embodied affective stances of interest, thereby signaling their collaboration. This joint (teacher–student) engagement in stancetaking is a form of co-regulation that acts as an indicator of the students' under-standing of appropriate behavior for this activity as well as their contribu-tion to the construction of the situation and its attendant mood. The children's understanding of appropriate ways to self-regulate their behavior is also evident when some of them whisper the word *fetch* to themselves by imitating Ms. Winter's voice (line 5.14), which creates a dialogic connec-tion with her stances. Here, the children self-regulate their behavior to enact both epistemic and affective stances that, in effect, demonstrate a stance of collaboration with their teacher. The children's regulatory actions and use of linguistic resources further contribute to the collabora-tive problem-solving mood.

This problem-solving mood is intensified when Ms. Winter has the children evaluate her spelling, asking, "does: this say↓:: fet↑::ch" with a thoughtful intonation and evenly metered cadence. Ms. Winter's affective stance attunes the children to the kinds of regulatory actions and degree of effort needed for successful engagement. The children respond in chorus with an emphatic "↑no::::" (line 5.23), an epistemic stance of reasonable certainty, as evidenced by the lengthening. Here, the children are actively co-regulating their behavior to collaborate in the ongoing interactive stancetak-ing, that is, the dance of stances. Through their interactional display, they co-regulate their behavior to align with the teacher on the same object (the word "fetch") as they maintain this emergent mood.

At this point, Ms. Winter responds with a disagreement that embodies a combination of stances. When she says, ">y↑::es ↑it do:es <- fe:tch: "

(lines 5.24–5.25), Ms. Winter simultaneously enacts an affective stance through patient prosody and an epistemic stance of certainty. Her certainty communicates to the children that if they do not pay close enough attention, they risk being wrong. At the same time, her stance of patience mitigates her potential displeasure and maintains the collaborative problem-solving mood. The implicit message here is that the children need to pay close attention, that is, they need to self-regulate their attention. Next, Ms. Winter asks the children, ">but is that the ↑right way to spell ↑it<." As a further form of mitigation, perhaps dismissing the previous question, her discourse marker "but" indicates that this question will contrast with her previous one. In this question, Ms. Winter shifts into a lower tone with a directive quality but continues to use a melodic prosody, indexing an epistemic stance of patient certainty. The students regulate their behaviors to co-participate in Ms. Winter's stances with another emphatic "no" (lines 5.31–5.33) thereby collectively indexing their own epistemic stance of certainty toward the "right way to spell" the word "fetch." In response, Ms. Winter aligns with the children by repeating their "no" as a marker of affirmation.

Taken as a whole, this sequential juxtaposition of stances builds a context in which the interlocutors (here, the teacher and the children) collaborate to maintain the mood (a problem-solving one, in this case) of the speaking event. Furthermore, this excerpt illustrates how participants (the students) both self- and co-regulate their behaviors in response to their teacher's stance. This dialogical dance between and within stances captures the complex ways that both adult and children interactively collaborate to create a contextual mood – one that influences the regulatory processes of these learners. Of course, it need not have happened this way; the children could have regulated their behaviors in ways to disaffirm the importance and seriousness of the work, which would have created an entirely different mood. Yet here the students did self- and co-regulate their behaviors to align with the teacher and, in so doing, they co-authored an emerging mood of engaged problem-solving. From a different angle, the teacher used affective and epistemic stancetaking to indicate the desired quality of the activity and the students used their stances to demonstrate their understandings of how to regulate appropriate engagement in learning.

Problem-Solving Mood and Collaboration

The next excerpt, Excerpt 5.2, which occurred immediately after Excerpt 5.1, demonstrates how, through the development of this problem-solving

Excerpt 5.2 *"does he n↑eed ta- gu↑e:ss"*

Ms. Winter:	=[because [↑<u>Andy</u>:: =	5.39
	[(((*a slight melodic quality*))	5.40
	[(((*Lifts up and looks at whiteboard and points to*	5.41
	"fech".))	5.42
	=[>at the en↑d =	5.43
	[(((*Continues with light melodic quality.*)) =of a	5.44
	[wor:[:d:- < (0.1) [(((*Looks at Andy.*))	5.45
Serge:	[(((*Lowers his arm.*))	5.46
Ms. Winter:	what three: letters:	5.47
	((*Looking at Andy and lifts white board and continued*	5.48
	slight melodic voice quality.))	5.49
	for the /ch:/ sound do we need for the <u>en:d</u> of a word.	5.50
	(0.3)	5.51
Students:	((*Turn back to look at Andy and then turn back to face to*	5.52
	Ms. Winter))	5.53
Victoria:	((*Raises her hand while looking at Ms. Winter.*))	5.54
Ms. Winter:	↑does he n↑eed ta- gu↑e:ss[:	5.55
	((*Slight melodic quality.*))	5.56
Alessandro:	[↑no	5.57
Student:	[no	5.58
Ms. Winter:	↑if he: for↑go:t	5.59
	((*Slight melodic quality with slightly lowered voice.*))	5.60
Students:	no::	5.61
Ms. Winter:	no::=	5.62

mood of engagement, the students were learning about specific forms of behavioral regulation for collaboration via their own and the teacher's stancetaking practices. In it, Ms. Winter pursues the still open question of how to properly spell the word "fetch." Utilizing a slight melodic prosody suggesting an affective stances of patience, Ms. Winter offers an explicit hint to direct the attention of a particular student, Andy, to "the en↑d of a wor::d" (lines 5.39–5.45). Continuing with a light melodic quality, Ms. Winter asks Andy to evaluate "what three: letters: for the / ch:/ sound do we need for the <u>en:d</u> of a word" (lines 5.47–5.50). These hints, delivered with a prosody indexing an affective stance of patience, maintain the epistemic stance of a serious request. The children, too, contribute to the seriousness and importance of the moment. Another student, Victoria, raises her hand, keen to provide an answer, while the rest of the class turns to look at Andy expectantly. Here then, the co-production of mood through stances is linked to self-regulatory processes. In other words, the self- and co-regulative behaviors of these children are both context-shaped and context-shaping.

Next, Ms. Winter poses another instructional question, this time directing it to the class as a whole, "↑does he n↑eed ta- gu↑e:ss:" (line 5.55). The yes/no phrasing of this question puts the students in the position of having to take an epistemic stance of certainty – either yes or no. Simultaneously, this question places the children in a position to evaluate what is needed to solve this particular problem. This is an implicit directive for when and how to self-regulate behavior when facing literacy problems in general. The children in this classroom, who know that guessing is discouraged in favor of tool/strategy use, collaborate in Ms. Winter's affective framing with an emphatic choral response of "no::" (line 5.61), suggesting a collective epistemic stance of certainty. This stance of certainty is confirmed by Ms. Winter who echoes "no" as a marker of agreement (line 5.62), affirming the appropriateness of a problem-solving strategy ("not guessing").

The stances taken by the teacher and students in this excerpt not only build the mood of collaborative engagement but also mark at least three appropriate ways to regulate behaviors for knowledge construction. First, the teacher's stances orient Andy and, by extension, the other students to the fact that one does not need to guess the answer, thus also suggesting that there is a different way to self-regulate behavior to figure out the answer. Second, the interactive stances reiterate the importance of collaboration through co-regulatory behaviors. Third, the teacher's patience in the emergence of this problem-solving mood can be appropriated (internalized) by the students to self-regulate their own engagement (see Holodynski, 2013).

Collaborative Problem-Solving Mood Sustained

In the prior interactional sequence, Ms. Winter oriented students to collaborative or co-regulate engagement. In Excerpt 5.3, which follows immediately after the previous one, Ms. Winter points to the importance of using tools (the classroom's sound cards) to offer help to peers (a co-regulatory behavior). The mood of collaborative engagement is further sustained through student and teacher stances.

This excerpt begins with Ms. Winter's question, "what car:d cou:ld he look at to: remember"(lines 5.63–5.65, 5.68). This question is delivered with metered melodic prosody, again indexing an affective stance of patience. This question entails the hint that he (Andy) could look at a sound card. Ms. Winter also enacts an epistemic stance by utilizing

Excerpt 5.3 *"nah: that's uh sh::ark"*

Ms. Winter:	=[what car:d cou:ld he look at.[=	5.63
	[((*Slight melodic quality with*	5.64
	slightly lowered voice.))	5.65
Student₁:	[/mm[::/ /da/ /ch:: /=	5.66
	((*Sounding out.*))	5.67
Ms. Winter:	= to[: remem: ↓ber	5.68
Serge:	[((*Turns head, looks at sound cards on back wall.*))	5.69
Bronte:	[((*Turns head, looks at sound cards on back wall.*))	5.70
Student₂:	car::d	5.71
Ms. Winter:	[Andy	5.72
Student₁:	[=/ch/ >↑chipmunk<	5.73
Student₃:	(em) S:: ↑chipmunk	5.74
Ms. Winter:	S↑:: H:	5.75
	[((*Looks up at the sound cards.*))	5.76
	is:[: that ↑uh chipmunk on the the /sch:/- S-H: car↑:d	5.77
	((*Slight melodic quality.*))	5.78
Student₄:	[((*Raises her hand, looking at Ms. Winter*))	5.79
Andy:	[((*Turns his head from looking at the sound cards that are*	5.80
	behind him.))	5.81
Student₅:	no[::	5.82
Ms. Winter:	[nah: that's uh sh::ark	5.83

a lowered intonation combined with a modal verb of possibility, "could," which somewhat softens the force of this question/hint (as compared with, for example, "what card should he look at to remember?"). Furthermore, by asking the entire class what card Andy could use, Ms. Winter implicates them in Andy's efforts to solve the problem. This is a subtle form of instruction for co-regulation that positions the children as *collaborative* agents while simultaneously indicating to them that it is acceptable, perhaps even desirable, to offer help to their fellow classmates. Again, Ms. Winter's stances maintain the collaborative problem-solving mood while also highlighting appropriate ways to regulate behavior for knowledge construction.

In this moment, the children do indeed regulate their behaviors to co-participate in this instructional process through their stances. They do this by collaborating through their embodied affective stances of interest combined with epistemic stances of certainty. Specifically, they turn to look in the direction of some sound cards (lines 5.69, 5.70); they echo the word "card" (line 5.71); and they say the /ch/ sound and the word chipmunk (lines 5.73, 5.74). Through these actions, the children regulate their behaviors to display an affective stance of interest and engage in what they have inferred as situationally appropriate behaviors. They are also using quiet vocal speech and gestures to coordinate (co-regulate) their attention, thought, and talk with Ms. Winter. In doing so, they help co-produce and maintain a mood of collaborative engagement, which solicits (demands) coordinated effort.

Next, when Ms. Winter overhears a student say the letter S (line 5.74), she herself gazes up at the sound cards and repeats these letters using a rising pitch contour indicative of a question (lines 5.75–5.76). This embodied stance of uncertainty accomplishes an implicit directive for the children to pay close attention to a specific sound card and its accompanying letters. Consequently, Ms. Winter's stance points to the student's answer as potentially *incorrect*. The implicit directive is heightened as Ms. Winter looks at the sound cards and asks the evaluation question, "is: that ↑uh chipmunk on the sch:–s-h: car:d" (line 5.77). Although Andy is still the focus of the conversation, Ms. Winter directs her questions to the entire class, again indicating the shared and collaborative nature of group work. The children again regulate their engagement with an affective stance of interest, responding with gestural and verbal actions that indicate their attentiveness to and understanding of Ms. Winter's evaluation question (lines 5.80–5.82). These dialogic productions of stances continue to create and sustain a mood that demands engagement, effort, and collaboration, all accomplished through regulatory processes of co- and self-regulation.

In Excerpt 5.4, Andy produces the desired answer, the letter combination "tch." The teacher, who does not hear his response at first, uses linguistic resources to sustain the serious mood. In addition to further illustrating the development of the mood, this excerpt shows how, through the use of an affective stance of impatience, Ms. Winter demonstrates what particular forms of collaborative engagement are appropriate in her class, that is, what forms of regulatory behaviors are needed for a collective problem-solving mood.

This excerpt begins as Andy is turning back from looking at the sound-spelling cards; he gazes up at Ms. Winter and says, "S:: ↑H:" (lines 5.85–5.87). Andy's movement and his slight rising intonation enact an epistemic stance of uncertainty as he coordinates his actions with Ms. Winter, who responds to him with a correction, "S:-H::. we just said. that's uh ↓sha:rk card:." Here Ms. Winter's voice has a down pitch contour that she typically used when children may not have paid close enough attention or did not remember specific aspects of a word or

Excerpt 5.4 *"we just said. [that's uh ↓sha:rk card"*

Andy:	[(((*Turning from looking at the sound cards to gaze at Ms.*	5.85
	Winter.))	5.86
	[S:: ↑H:	5.87
Ms. Winter:	S:: H::. ↑we just said. [that's uh ↓sha:rk card. we	5.88
	went /ch::./	5.89
Andy:	[(((*Turns head back to look up at*	5.90
	the sound cards.))	5.91
	[uhm: °T::°- >CH<	5.92
	[(((*Turning back to look at Ms. Winter, raises arm up and snaps*	5.93
	his wrist.))	5.94
Students:	((*Raising hands.*))	5.95
Ms. Winter:	hum↑::	5.96
Andy:	C ↑ H	5.97
Ms. Winter:	>it already< ha:z uh- C::H[=	5.98
		5.99
Students:	[(((*Students raise hands quickly,*	5.100
	some look at sound cards.))	5.101
	[oo:: oo::	5.102
	[(((*Excited voices.*))	5.103
Ms. Winter:	[=but=	5.104
Elijah:	[(((*Leans toward Andy and whispers at his back.*))	5.105
	[°T C H°	5.106
Andy:	[(((*Looks back and up at sound cards.*))	5.107
Ms. Winter:	=↑this is the >↑en::d. of the word<- so this is >gonna< be	5.108
	wr:[↓ong:: ((*slight melodic prosody*))	5.109
Andy:	[°T::: >C-H<°	5.110
	[(((*Turns toward Ms. Winter, whispering.*))	5.111
Students:	[°T:: C-H°	5.112
	[(((*Looking at the sound cards whispering letters.*))	5.113
Ms. Winter:	>put yur< han::ds: dow:n:. – un unless your name is Andy	5.114
	((*Slightly melodic prosody; softer tone.*))	5.115

lesson, producing an affective stance of impatience. In combination with her epistemic stance of certainty ("↑we just said.", line 5.88) and her implicit appraisal of "not knowing," Ms. Winter sustains the seriousness of the mood.

In keeping with this mood, Andy turns to look at the sound cards again and then turns to look up at Ms. Winter and says "uhm°T::°- >CH<" in a quiet voice (lines 5.90–5.94), enacting an epistemic stance of uncertainty. When Ms. Winter says "hum," Andy alters his response and says the letters "C, H" a bit louder (line 5.97). Ms. Winter responds to this self-repair by saying, "it already< ha:z uh- C H but ↑this is the >↑en::d. of the word<- so this is >gonna< be wr:ong::." Although she enacts an epistemic stance of certainty in this evaluation, "this is ... wrong," Ms. Winter now uses a slightly melodic prosody to enact an affective stance of patience but combines it with a lowered pitch to indicate the seriousness of a "wrong" response. Across this data set, Ms. Winter combines epistemic and affective stances in this way during evaluative talk to encourage a child to continue thinking/responding and maintain a problem-solving mood.

Now, hearing the implied evaluation of "wrong," the children as a group begin to coordinate and align with Ms. Winter through stances that are both affective (excited) and epistemic (knowing that one must look at the sound-spelling cards to generate correct responses). The children's enthusiastic raising of their hands and their audible cries of "ooh ooh" indicate not only that they think they have the answer but that having the right answer is something to be excited about. This suggests that collaborative problem-solving moods influence children's perceptions of what is of value, that is, what matters to them and others around them.

Ms. Winter responds with a strong directive, ">put yur< han::ds: dow: n:.- un unless your name is Andy" (lines 5.114–5.115). The epistemic stance of certainty in this directive is accomplished through a flat pitch contour and an evenly metered rhythm. This stance is now combined with a noticeably softer voice quality and the melodic prosody of Ms. Winter's patient stances. On the surface, her strong directive contradicts what the children were expected to do earlier, that is, regulate their behaviors to evaluate and give help. The children, however, were not helping Andy identify the correct tool but rather providing the answer. Here again, Ms. Winter's sanctioning of the students functions as a subtle form of instruction that lets them know what kinds of helping behaviors are appropriate to this situation and this mood. She is also implicitly indicating that help giving means regulating behavior to assist peers with the *correct use of tools*, not merely providing correct answers.

In the final excerpt, Ms. Winter and Andy go over the approach that Andy used to generate his correct answer. Together they co-produce an explication of how to use the sound-spelling cards to determine the spelling of phonemes at the end of a word. This interaction demonstrates how Ms. Winter taught children to engage in instructional explanations as forms of co-regulation. In fact, affective and epistemic stances are combined to coordinate the entire group. The children, who have responded to Ms. Winter's tonal shifts by quieting down and paying close attention, are part of a collaborative multiparty affective stance of interest toward Ms.

Excerpt 5.5 *"an:d howdaya know it's uh ↑T:: C::H:."*

Andy:	T::: >C:H<	5.116
Ms. Winter:	[an:d howdaya know it's uh ↑T:: . > C::H:.<	5.117
	[*((slight melodic prosody continued softer tone))*	5.118
	[*((writing on the board and then looks up at Andy))*	5.119
Andy:	because I loo:ked up- dhis:- car::d	5.120
Ms. Winter:	an: >what duh< why >would it be <- why would it be	5.121
	[T::C::H::- instead of ↑C::H	5.122
	[*((slight melodic prosody, soft tone))*	5.123
Andy:	[because it has uh gree:n. bo:x	5.124
	[*((Glances back at the cards and then back to Ms. Winter.))*	5.125
Ms. Winter:	becau:se: ↑this: >wou:ld be:< like the green box- right	5.126
	here:: [(0.2) *((Slight melodic prosody, soft tone))*	5.127
	[*((Drawing a green box around TCH at the end of*	5.128
	a vocabulary word; light melodic prosody.))	5.129
Students:	*((Quietly looking up at the teacher.))*	5.130
Ms. Winter:	and then: you- put T:::- C::- H:.	5.131
	[*((Drawing a square around the letters of prior words,*	5.132
	soft tone.))	5.133
	[this: would be like: the gree:n box- her:e::- [l:: u::-=	5.134
	[*((slight melodic prosody/soft tone))* [*((Taps on*	5.135
	letters L, U))	5.136
	=and [then- the ↑C:K:. Kay one more::: wo::rd	5.137
	[*((Draws a line underneath the letter C-K and then*	5.138
	looks at Andy.))	5.139
	[*((Slight melodic prosody, soft tone.)*	5.140

Winter's and Andy's explanation of how to determine the spelling of the /
ch/ phoneme at the end of a word.

Here, Andy is restating his response, "T::: >C-H<" (line 5.116). Unlike
his earlier uncertainty about the answer, Andy's response is now given with
emphatic stress, marking an epistemic stance of certainty. Ms. Winter's
reply is in the form of an evaluation question, "howda you know it's uh
>↑t:: . c::h:.<" (line 5.117). Her reply contains an up pitch contour and
melodic prosody that index the patient stance she took in her initial
instructional questions. The voice quality in Ms. Winter's response, however, is noticeably softer. This softness in combination with an affective
stance of patience is the way that Ms. Winter used linguistic resources to
indicate that she was sharing information that all the children in the class
needed to learn. Interestingly, in this instance, it is Andy's solution to the
problem, i.e., how *he* knew the spelling was "tch" at the end of a word, that
is marked as important information to know. Ms. Winter explicitly

accomplishes this by asking Andy "why would it be 'tch' instead of 'ch'" while utilizing an affective stance of patience (lines 5.121–5.123). Through these stances, the meaning of this local collaborative problem-solving mood becomes more elaborated; students are positioned as agential and competent actors who can self-regulate their behavior to collaboratively produce knowledge.

Andy's response is an embodied epistemic stance of certainty toward his own knowledge and toward the use of the sound cards. His stance is accomplished through the self-regulation of both movement (glancing at the sound cards to confirm what he saw) and utterances ("because it has uh gree:n. bo:x"). Ms. Winter implicitly evaluates Andy's response as accurate and important information to know when she utilizes part of Andy's answer to further elaborate his response (lines 5.126–5.129). She goes on to repeat this stance as she draws a green box around the letters "tch" to point out what students need to pay attention to when using the sound-spelling cards as a literacy tool (lines 5.126–5.129). Ms. Winter concludes by looking up at Andy, confirming the importance of his correct response.

In this chapter, we presented a series of excerpts to document how a contextual mood (here, a collaborative problem-solving mood) emerges over time as a communicative, collaborative, and relational process through stancetaking. Through the micro organization of talk, the interlocutors in this learning context regulated their behaviors to coordinate their affective and epistemic stances dialogically and opportunistically to build a meaningful context. The context they constructed was *not* a neutral field of action. Their collaborative and coordinated social acts/stances filled the situation with a mood that solicited, even demanded, that they regulate their behaviors to engage in joint attention, effortful listening, memory, correct tool use, and collaboration. In other words, the collaborative problem-solving mood demanded particular forms of behavior regulation. In this way, co- and self-regulatory behaviors were inherently related to the processes involved in mood creation. In turn, the mood became constitutive not only of the social processes of learning but also of the historically built social context, which then functioned as a resource, that is, a contextual affordance. The children used this resource to interpret the emergent mood; accordingly, they opportunistically and agentially regulated their behaviors. In sum, mood emerged out of the affective and epistemic stances taken by the teacher and the students. This mood then suggested how students ought to properly regulate their behavior to enact their roles (statuses) within this collaborative mood. In turn, the collaborative mood indicated appropriate involvement (e.g., giving answers to questions about *how* to solve the problem). It is through such historical and in-the-moment interactional processes of stancetaking, we contend, that mood becomes an inherent part of educational contexts and influences the ways children regulate their behaviors for engagement in learning.

We have demonstrated that mood is more than any single instance of stance. Of course, understanding an emerging mood requires that we attend to the stances taken by interactants. Yet, while stance is an extremely useful tool for understanding the subtle and implicit work that is going on, it is not enough. In order to fully grasp the meaning and the effect of interactional work, researchers and educators must study the back and forth of stancetaking across time, revealing the elaborate network of relations between participants and objects and activities, that is, the emergent mood of a social context. In the case of Ms. Winter's classroom, it was essential to consider how the teacher's and the students' stancetaking practices were used to jointly build a contextual mood. The students did not have to follow along – they could have paid little or no attention to their teacher. But they did follow along, regulating their behaviors to take a stance of active interest, collaborating and helping each other as asked. Through all of this interactive stancetaking and regulatory work, a collaborative and engaged problem-solving mood emerged.

Following Silver (2011), we contend that situational mood *does* something to interactional participants. Specifically, it functions as an affective-volitional (motivational) process. In Andy's case, mood helped him regulate his behavior (e.g., staying attentive and focused over time) in ways that he might not otherwise have been able to do. This points to the significance of moods in contexts where activities are designed to foster learning beyond a child's current level of competency, that is, zones of proximal development (Vygotsky, 1978). Zones of proximal development present children with a range of motivational challenges involving the regulation of attention, memory, effortful engagement, and the like. The study of contextual mood has the potential to show how such challenges are influenced by the interactional co-creation of a learning activity over time. Consequently, we argue that it is important to examine the crucial role that moods play in structuring children's learning and developmental processes. For these reasons, and because moods are so impactful on how learners regulate their behaviors, thereby influencing what learners accomplish, we see contextual mood as a particularly important construct for practitioners as well as researchers. Teachers, for example, could harness the concept of mood to create contexts that better help learners engage in challenging activities and also persist in the face of difficulty.

This chapter presents what we believe is one of the first detailed descriptions of how classroom moods emerge and influence the regulatory processes of learning. Yet because moods are holistic phenomena, because they are not straightforwardly decomposable into parts and because they are not equal to the sum of their parts, observing or studying the role of contextual mood in influencing regulatory processes is a challenging endeavor. Still, engaging in this endeavor can reveal how regulatory processes and feelings become intertwined in the cognitive activities that foster optimal learning; and, understanding this process can help educators, in and out of school, design social contexts in which learners thrive to engage those regulatory processes that lead to the development of complex cognitive functions during learning events.

Conclusion

We began this book with a deep concern about understanding the relationship between cultural contexts, human learning and development, and behavioral regulation. This concern moved us away from more traditional views of the individual as an isolated entity who controls and self-directs engagement toward seeing individuals as agential beings who regulate behaviors in relation with their social and material worlds. This shift in perspective reflects an appreciation for the profoundly unique contributions of Vygotsky's (1978) cultural-historical developmental theory and its treatment of semiotic resources as devices used and created by agents to control, direct, and solicit psychological and pragmatic behaviors. To capture how the semiotic regulation of behavior during learning is enacted as an individual, collaborative, and social process, we combined Vygotskian theory with the complementary intellectual disciplines of linguistic anthropology (Duranti & Goodwin, 1992; Kockelman, 2006, 2012; Ochs, 1990, 1993), cultural psychology (Cole, 1996, 1995; Dewey, 1938; Engeström, 1999; Mead, 1934/1962; Valsiner, 2001), and sociology (Bourdieu, 1977, 1985; Sacks, Schegloff, & Jefferson, 1974). This interdisciplinary approach provides sophisticated conceptual and methodological tools for creating a set of sociocultural lenses for observing and analyzing how learning practices and agential individuals within these practices organize behavioral regulation over long and short periods of time. The purpose of these lenses is to rethink behavioral regulation as an inherently cultural, relational, and agential process through which cognitive and social-emotional competencies develop.

In our sociocultural approach, self-regulation continues to be an indicator of higher mental functions, that is, an indicator of psychological competencies for controlling intellectual and affective behaviors (Vygotsky, 1978). But we reframe self-regulation as only one part of a whole system of regulatory processes that functions as an indicator of competence, a competency that is also interactively used by active learners to co-create and co-author their psychological competencies, their identities, and their social and cultural learning contexts. This system of behavioral regulation is not used in a lockstep way in learning activities but rather is dynamic, relational, and ever-evolving, particularly when engaged in the complexities of real-world learning processes that foster learning and development in all participants. Most importantly, this complex process of behavioral regulation nurtures learners when it emerges from agential activities and the creative and habitual transactions of agents who carry out as well as create these activities.

Of course, regulatory processes emerging in the flurry of learning activities are complicated and difficult to recognize, not least because engagement in learning practices influences behavioral regulation and shapes our cognitive, affective, and social worlds. The sociocultural lenses in each of the preceding chapters are designed to offer a set of analytical tools to "see" how regulatory processes are inherently interconnected with the social and material context, with the ultimate goal of revealing how they emerge in and are structured by the relational, cognitive, and moral acts of doing, being, and knowing. We utilize the generative power of sociocultural theories to conceptualize, develop, and refine four different but complementary analytical tools for revealing how individuals' engagement in different aspects of a practice influence behavioral regulation in learning activity: relational habitus, practical-moral knowledge, identity of competency, and contextual mood. These four analytical tools foreground the individual within the ecology of a social, semiotic, and cultural context of learning. We recognize that this set of conceptual tools does not capture all of the complex ways in which behavioral regulation is situationally organized and emerges during sense-making with others. Nevertheless, taken as an ensemble of resources, these sociocultural frames provide a powerful means of seeing contextual influences that are otherwise difficult to discern, whether for participants engaged in activity or for those who study such engagement.

In an effort to integrate how these analytical tools can be of practical value for educators, students, and researchers alike, we will briefly summarize the concepts and claims from the preceding chapters. First, however, it is important to acknowledge that at the core of our claims is the assumption that culture and individuals are constitutive of one another. The co-production of self and culture happens in every place where people regulate practical, moral, social, and psychological behaviors to become competent members of their communities. Most importantly, through these regulatory processes, people become agents when they are treated as if they can do something of their own volition, that is, intentionally decide on an action and enact that action whether by oneself or in concert with others (see Berducci, 2004; Kockelman, 2012). The emergence and development of agency in everyday practices is fundamental to all forms of behavioral regulation, self-, other-, co-, and socially shared regulation.

The process of developing into an agential being starts very early in life and continues to develop through engagement in proleptic activities, which evoke "the future in the present" (Flynn, 1991) by treating novices or learners as competent, intentional agents who can control and direct their learning behavior in collaboration with others. Take, for example, an infant pointing at and reaching for a toy. When a caregiver interprets this as a self-regulated request and hands the object to the infant, meaning is imputed to the action and the infant is treated as volitional/intentional, even if this particular competency has yet to develop. Over time, repeated proleptic experiences in learning situations foster agency as well as meaning-making as a social and relational competency that includes all forms of behavioral regulation. What is more, the development of this competency shifts control over cognitive processes such as attention, memory, problem-solving, and reasoning from the external pressures or support of caregivers, teachers, or mentors to the self-directive inclinations of active agents. This shift is important in supporting an agent's own interest in activity, which begins to guide engagement and thereby plays a critical role in fostering individuals' desires and motivations to utilize a system of regulatory processes with others.

There is little doubt that prolepsis is an important element of what we have referred to as *agential activity* in that it creates opportunity spaces for novices to act on and affect their world and themselves. Through this engagement, novices develop relational, social, and semiotic competencies for self-, other-, co-, and socially shared regulation. Such competencies are embedded in real-world contexts, which are themselves influenced by and influential on social agents. To understand the influence of local contexts, we explain how and why the use of a "practice" lens is helpful in viewing regulatory processes in social situations (Chapter 1). This lens brings together a historical and dynamic view of context as emerging from the ongoing interactive construction of agential activity through communicative resources. Furthermore, focusing on agential activities makes it possible to see how agents (whether learners, novices, or mentors/educators) shape their future by utilizing the inherent affordances and constraints of the emerging and historical context to control and direct their engagement in routine activities. In effect, a social practice lens highlights the importance of understanding regulatory processes as originating from engagement in contextually situated meaningful, goal-directed activities of a local community. The structure of agential activities in a community solicits (an affordance) and directs (a constraint) behavior toward the local values/norms, moral codes of conduct, and valued identities, all of which influences how learners and others decide to regulate their behaviors.

Understanding the complexity and ambiguity of contextual, social, and relational influences on regulatory processes in a practice is not a simple task but it is aided by the activity theoretic mediational triangle explained in Chapter 1. The meditational triangle of cultural-historical activity theory (CHAT) as a simplified diagram of a cultural practice makes obvious those aspects of engagement in activities that are often implicit or taken for granted – for example, how intellectual labor such as who defines instructional problems or who directs thinking is divided between mentor and learner. The power of the CHAT model is that it can be used by students and research practitioners as an analytical tool to study cognitive, social-emotional, or meaning-making processes in learning contexts. This same model can also be used by educators as a conceptual tool to make aspects of their instructional practice explicit, observable, and thereby open to reflection and potential improvement.

Complementing CHAT's mediational triangle is the relational habitus (RH), explained in Chapter 2. The RH offers a means of observing and better understanding the spontaneous, creative, and habitual ways that agential learners utilize the system of behavioral regulation actions during the intersubjective processes of meaning-making. Observing these intersubjective processes over time reveals how learners in a local context develop particular forms of behavioral regulation as "cultural habits" of engagement (Vygotsky, 1929). In learning communities, these habits represent a repertoire of valued ways of regulating behavior with others as part of an ecological arrangement including tools and tasks. The local organization of an RH also reveals how learners integrate the social with the creative and authored self by utilizing semiotic resources (affordances) to control and direct attention, memory, perception, emotion, imagination, and problem-solving in qualitatively new ways. Within an RH, these new ways of regulating psychological and practical behaviors can be attributed to a distributed mind (rather than an individual one) emerging from relational, agential, and creative (transformative) ways of being in the world.

Relational, agential, and creative ways of being and making sense are also attached to moral meanings. Chapter 3, on practical-moral knowledge

(PMK), offers a conceptual tool for seeing how engagement in different forms of behavioral regulation within an RH is not a "free market and benign" process but rather inherently connected to the moral meanings constructed in a local context (Goodnow, 1990). The historical and emergent construction of a social context creates PMK as a socially shared semiotic (sign) system of rights, responsibilities, and duties. This form of knowledge exists in any learning context, whether formal or informal, and it exerts a powerful influence over regulatory processes by nurturing, expecting, and even demanding who can do what, when, where, and how. Learners draw from and create this knowledge as they learn to regulate behaviors to accomplish tasks. Likewise, PMK helps learners determine and assess who has the right to engage in the construction of knowledge or what feelings toward learning are appropriate and when these rights are in play. In this sense, PMK distributes power, responsibilities, and duties for particular regulated actions in both symmetrical and asymmetrical ways. Learners accordingly develop a repertoire of social actions for regulating behavior that represents moral ways of being valued in a local context. The lens we offer for PMK offers one approach for researchers and students who are interested in studying how everyday regulated social actions and interactions during learning can be conceptualized in moral terms; and, for practitioners, utilizing the PMK lens as an observational and reflective tool can help them in designing instructional activities for productive engagement in small- or whole-group learning such that learners co-participate in becoming active agents in their own learning and active agents in their own developing competencies.

As Wenger (1998) points out, "our definition of competence shape(s) our identities" (p. 193) and influences the ways we participate in learning. To explain how this definition exerts an influence over learners and their engagement in a system of regulatory processes, we offer identities of competency as an analytical lens in Chapter 4. These identities emerge and develop over time in learning settings from locally negotiated thoughts and ideas about what constitutes competency, whether explicitly or implicitly recognized and expressed. Regardless of how these ideas emerge, they become constitutive of a socially shared category for competency. Because this social category is constructed and continually develops in local settings, it can vary within and across all learning arenas. Nonetheless, it is this shared and continually evolving category that exerts a powerful influence over engagement as it is used by learners in the construction of a highly desired but often implicit social identity. When learners regulate their behaviors to enact those actions and interactions associated with competency, they are indexing or pointing to competent ways of doing and being valued in their community, that is, the socially shared category of competency. Through this indexical process, learners are actively trying to attach themselves to, and take up recognizable incumbency in, this social category (Bowker & Star, 1999; Hall, 2004). Through these efforts, they are vying to inhabit a locally constructed identity of competency, even though this is a non-articulated form of identity. An identity of competency is of enormous importance for engagement in learning in that it functions as an emerging sense of self as competent. And, in learning contexts, research has shown that a sense of self as competent results in regulated behaviors that display being motivated to learn and display a willingness to sustain this motivation (Elliot & Dweck, 2005). These behaviors have a significant influence on what a learner develops over time and how their engagement in learning processes is perceived and evaluated.

The same actions and interactions used to inhabit an identity of competency also represent a proleptic activity/practice of creating the future-in-the-present by regulating behavior to enact competency in the present even though it is still emerging. Through this process, learners make the effort to use semiotic resources to control their thinking and feelings as they are actively utilizing those actions, interactions, strategies, skills, thoughts, and ideas associated with competency. Thus, by vying for an identity of competency, learners are helping to shape agential activities as they shape their future. By being aware of this process, researchers and students can investigate how learners use different configurations of self-, co-, other- and socially shared regulated behaviors to inhabit and display their emerging academic and knowledge construction competencies. Of course, practitioners can use this analytical tool to help inform their design of instructional contexts that foster sustained engagement in complex learning and problem-solving.

All experiences in learning contexts, whether vying for and inhabiting a social identity, constructing new understandings, or using/generating practical-moral knowledge to regulate behaviors, are charged with emotions and feelings, or what Vygotsky (1934/1986) termed perezhivanie, that is, the emotional experience of a situation. In Chapter 5, we offer the notion of a *contextual mood* to account for the flow and influence of emergent feelings during learning and their relationship to behavioral regulation in social contexts. Because contextual moods are distributed across time and space, they are better viewed as a social and emergent phenomenon that exist both beyond and between individuals' minds; and, contextual moods are not simply experienced by individuals but rather by collectives, such as whole or small groups engaged in activity. Individuals within these collectives bring contextual moods into existence through the back-and-forth interactional context of communicative events by controlling and directing their use of two linguistic resources: affective and epistemic stances. As individuals use linguistic stances in spontaneous, creative, and unexpected ways, contextual moods emerge and, most importantly, solicit particular ways of regulating behaviors for engagement in learning. Becoming aware of how contextual moods emerge and how they influence engagement in regulatory processes offers a different way of viewing the relationship between feelings and engagement in cognitive activities.

Across all of our analytical frames, we have painted a picture of regulatory processes as part of dynamic, complex, spontaneous, and relational processes of context creating and context using. Contexts from this perspective are relational and within these contexts, the micro relationships of self, tools, tasks, and others (the RH) organize the meaning-making processes that foster intellectual and social-emotional learning and development. By utilizing the RH as a way to conceptualize and "see" behavioral regulation, we moved beyond methodological individualism to the social and meaningful ways we co-construct psychological and practical competencies. This approach reframed self-regulation as only one part of a system of regulatory processes – a system that is always socially situated and always reflective of local perspectives about competency and how to gain it and how to display it. It is our hope that the sociocultural frames described in this book can be used as tools to contribute to research about regulatory processes as they emerge in the relational and social interactional constitution of our social selves, our social world, and our psychological competencies. For practitioners especially, we hope these analytical frames offer the potential to create intellectual opportunities for what Dewey (2002) calls *reflective agency*, or improving practice through "critical curiosity, thoughtfulness, and tolerance to new ideas" (as cited in Whipple, 2005, p. 162). By Dewey's account, reflective agency fosters the development of transformative habits that enables the continual improvement, refinement, and reorganization of instructional practices, the result of which is ideally the development of productive and positive intellectual and social-emotional competencies for learners.

References

Allal, L. (2011). Pedagogy, didactics and the co-regulation of learning: A perspective from the French-language world of educational research. *Research Papers in Education*, 26(3), 329–336.

Alter, C. (2018). The school shooting generation has had enough. *Time*, March 22. http://time.com/longform/never-again-movement

Atkinson, J. M. & Heritage, J. (1984). *Structures of Social Action: Studies in Conversation Analysis*. Cambridge: Cambridge University Press.

Bakhtin, M. M. (1986). *Speech Genres and Other Late Essays* (V. McGee, Trans.). Austin: University of Texas Press.

Barad, K. (2007). *Quantum Physics and the Entanglement of Matter and Meaning*. Durham, NC: Duke University Press.

Biber, D. & Finegan, E. (1989). Styles of stance in English: Lexical and grammatical marking of evidentiality and affect. *Text*, 9(1), 93–124.

Blumer, H. (1969). *Symbolic Interactionism: Perspective and Method*. Berkeley: University of California Press.

Blunden, A. (2010). *An Interdisciplinary Theory of Activity*. Leiden: Brill.

Boekaerts, M. (2001). Context sensitivity: Activated motivational beliefs, current concerns, and emotional arousal. In S. Volet & S. Järvelä (Eds.), *Motivation in Learning Contexts: Theoretical Advances and Methodological Implications* (pp. 17–32). Elmsford, NY: Pergamon Press.

Bourdieu, P. (1977). *Outline of a Theory of Practice*. New York: Cambridge University Press.

Bourdieu, P. (1980). *The Logic of Practice* (R. Nice, Trans.). Stanford: Stanford University Press.

Bourdieu, P. (1985). The genesis of the concepts of habitus and field. *Sociocriticism*, 2, 11–24.

Bowker, G. & Star, S. L. (1999). *Sorting Things Out: Classification and Its Consequences*. Cambridge, MA: MIT Press.

Bruner, J. (1996). *The Culture of Education*. Cambridge: Cambridge University Press.

Campbell Bartoletti, S. (1999). *Kids on Strike!* New York: Houghton Mifflin Harcourt.

Children's Crusade (n.d.). National Civil Rights Museum, Memphis, TN.

Chizhik, A. W. (2001). Equity and status in group collaboration: Learning through explanations depends on task characteristics. *Social Psychology of Education*, 5(2), 179–200.

Cohen, J. L. (2008). "That's not treating you as a professional": Teachers constructing complex professional identities through talk. *Teachers and Teaching: Theory and Practice*, 14(2), 79–93.

Cohen, J. L. (2010). Getting recognized: Teachers negotiating professional identities as learners through talk. *Teacher and Teacher Education*, 26(3), 473–481.

Cole, M. (1995). The supra-individual envelope of development: Activity and practice, situation and context. In J. Goodnow, P. Miller, & F. Kessel (Eds.), *Cultural Practices as Contexts for Development* (pp. 105–118). San Francisco: Jossey-Bass

Cole, M. (1996). *Cultural Psychology: A Once and Future Discipline*. Cambridge, MA: Harvard University Press.

Cole, M. (2003). Culture and cognitive growth. *Outlines*, 1, 3–15.

Cole, M. (2005). Cultural-historical activity theory in the family of socio-cultural approaches. *International Society for the Study of Behavioral Development Newsletter*, 29(3), 1–4.

Daniels, H. (2015). Mediation: An expansion of the socio-cultural gaze. *History of the Human Sciences*, 28(2), 34–50.

de Bruin, A. B. H. & van Gog, T. (2012). Improving self-monitoring and self-regulation: From cognitive psychology to the classroom. *Learning and Instruction*, 22(4), 245–252.

Dent, A. L. & Koenka, A. C. (2016). The relation between self-regulated learning and academic achievement across childhood and adolescence: A meta-analysis. *Educational Psychology Review*, 28(3), 425–474.

Devos, T. & Banaji, M. B. (2003). Implicit self and identity. In M. R. Leary & J. P. Tangney (Eds.), *Handbook of Self and Identity* (pp. 153–175). New York: Guilford Press.

Dewey, J. (1938). *Experience and Education*. New York: Macmillan.

Dewey, J. (1929/1958). *Experience and Nature*. Mineola, NY: Dover Publications.

Dewey, J. (2002). *Human Nature and Conflict*. Mineola, NY: Dover Publications.

Dings, R. (2018). Understanding phenomenological differences in how affordances solicit action: An exploration. *Phenomenology and the Cognitive Sciences*, 17(4), 681–699.

Do, S. L. & Schallert, D. L. (2004). Emotions and classroom talk: Toward a model of the role of affect in students' experiences of classroom discussions. *Journal of Educational Psychology*, 96(4), 619–634.

Du Bois, J. W. (2007). The stance triangle. In R. Englebretson (Ed.), *Stancetaking in Discourse: The Intersubjectivity of Interaction* (pp. 139–182). Amsterdam: John Benjamins.

Duranti, A. (2010). Husserl, intersubjectivity and anthropology. *Anthropological Theory*, 10(1–2), 16–35.

Duranti, A. & Goodwin, C. (Eds.). (1992). *Rethinking Context: Language as an Interactive Phenomena*. New York: Cambridge University Press.

Edwards, D. & Mercer, N. (1987). *Common Knowledge: The Development of Understanding in the Classroom.* New York: Methuen.

Elliot, A. J. & Dweck, C. S. (Eds.). (2005). *Handbook of Competence Motivation.* New York: Guilford Press.

Ellis, B. D. & Stam, J. H. (2015). Crisis? What crisis? Cross-cultural psychology's appropriation of cultural psychology. *Culture & Psychology, 21*(3), 293–317.

Ellis, R. (2003). *Task-Based Language Learning and Teaching.* New York: Oxford University Press.

Engeström, Y. (1999). Activity theory and individual and social transformation. In Y. Engeström, R. Miettinen, & R. L. Punamäki (Eds.), *Perspectives on Activity Theory* (pp. 19–38). New York: Cambridge University Press.

Engeström, Y. (2008). Enriching activity theory without shortcuts. *Interacting with Computers, 20*(2), 256–259.

Fields, D. & Enyedy, N. (2013). Picking up the mantle of "expert": Assigned roles, assertion of identity, and peer recognition. *Mind, Culture, and Activity, 20*(2), 113–131.

Flynn, P. J. (1991). *The Ethnomethodological Movement.* New York: De Gruyter Mouton.

Forgas, J. P., Baumeister, R. F., & Tice, D. M. (2009). The psychology of self regulation: An introductory review. In J. P. Forgas, R. F. Baumeister, & D. M. Tice (Eds.), *Psychology of Self Regulation: Cognitive, Affective, and Motivational Processes* (Vol. 11, pp. 1–17). New York: Psychology Press.

Fuhs, M. W., Farran, D. C., & Nesbitt, K. T. (2013). Preschool classroom processes as predictors of children's cognitive self-regulation skills development. *School Psychology Quarterly, 28*(4), 347–359.

Garfinkel, H. (1967). *Studies in Ethnomethodology.* Malden, MA: Blackwell.

Gee, J. P. (2000). Identity as an analytical lens for research in education. *Review of Research in Education, 25*, 99–125.

Getzels, J. W. (1975). Problem-finding and the inventiveness of solutions. *Journal of Creative Behavior, 9*(1), 12–18.

Gibson, J. J. (1969). *Principles of Perceptual Learning and Development.* New York: Appleton-Century-Crofts.

Gibson, J. J. (1986). *The Ecological Approach to Visual Perception.* Hillsdale, NJ: Lawrence Erlbaum.

Gilmore, K. (2014). The Birmingham Children's Crusade of 1963. February 14. www.biography.com/news/black-history-birmingham-childrens-crusade-1963-video

Goffman, E. (1974). *An Essay on the Organization of Experience: Frame Analysis.* Boston: Northeastern University Press.

Göncü, A. (1993). *The Senses Considered as Perceptual Systems.* Boston: Houghton Mifflin.

Goodnow, J. (1990). The socialization of cognition: What's involved? In J. W. Stigler, R. A. Shweder, & G. Herdt (Eds.), *Cultural Psychology: Essays on Comparative Human Development* (pp. 259–286). New York: Cambridge University Press.

Goodnow, J. & Lawrence, J. (2015). Children and cultural context. In M. Bornstein, T. Leventhal, & R. M. Lerner (Eds.), *Handbook of Child Psychology and Developmental Science. Volume 4: Ecological Settings and Processes* (7th ed.). Hoboken, NJ: John Wiley & Sons.

Goodwin, C. (2007). Participation, stance, and affect in the organization of activities. *Discourse & Society, 18*(1), 53–73.

Griffin, P. & Cole, M. (1984). Current activity for the future: The zo-ped. In B. Rogoff & J. Wertsch (Eds.), *New Directions for Child Development* (Vol. 23, pp. 45–63). San Francisco: Jossey-Bass.

Haag, M. (2018). Two workers at Arizona migrant children centers are charged with sexual abuse. *New York Times*, August 3. www.nytimes.com/2018/08/03/us/sexual-abuse-arizona-migrant-children.html

Hadwin, A. & Oshige, M. (2011). Self-regulation, coregulation, and socially-shared regulation: Exploring perspectives of self-regulated learning theory. *Teachers College Record, 113*(2), 240–264.

Hall, R. (2004). Attaching self and others to social categories as an interactional and historical achievement. *Human Development, 47,* 354–360.

Harmon-Jones, C., Bastian, B., & Harmon-Jones, E. (2016). The discrete emotions questionnaire: A new tool for measuring state self-report emotions. *PLoS One, 11*(8), 1–25.

Heritage, J. (1984). A change of state token and aspects of it sequential placement. In J. M. Atkinson & J. C. Heritage (Eds.), *Structures of Social Action: Studies in Conversational Analysis* (pp. 299–345). Cambridge: Cambridge University Press.

Holland, D. & Cole, M. (1995). Between discourse and schema: Reformulating a cultural-historical approach to culture and mind. *Anthropology and Education Quarterly, 26*(4), 475–490.

Holland, D. & Lachicotte, W. J. (2007). Vygotsky, Mead, and the new socio-cultural studies of identity. In H. Daniels, M. Cole, & J. V. Wertsch (Eds.), *The Cambridge Companion to Vygotsky* (pp. 101–135). Cambridge: Cambridge University Press.

Holodynski, M. (2013). The internalization theory of emotion: A cultural-historical approach to the development of emotions. *Mind, Culture, and Activity, 20*(1), 4–38.

Hutchins, E. (1991). The social organization of distributed cognition. In L. B. Resnick, J. M. Levine, & S. D. Teasely (Eds.), *Perspectives on Socially Shared Cognition*. Washington, DC: American Psychology Association.

Iiskala, T., Vauras, M., Lehtinen, E., & Salonen, P. (2011). Socially-shared metacognition of dyads of pupils in collaborative mathematical problem solving. *Learning and Instruction, 21*(3), 379–393.

Jaffe, A. (2009). *Stance: Sociolinguistic perspectives*. New York: Oxford University Press.

Janlert, L. & Stolterman, E. (1997). The character of things. *Design Studies, 18,* 297–314.

Kärkkäinen, E. (2003). *Epistemic Stance in English Conversation*. Amsterdam: John Benjamins.

Kärkkäinen, E. (2004). Interactional practices and linguistic resources of stance taking in spoken English. In J. O. Östman (Ed.), *PIC Bulletin 7* (pp. 45–48). Helsinki: University of Helsinki.

Kirschner, S. & Martin, J. (Eds.). (2010). *The Sociocultural Turn in Psychology: The Contextual Emergence of Mind and Self.* New York: Columbia University Press.

Knappett, C. (2005). *Thinking Through Material Culture: An Interdisciplinary Perspective.* Philadelphia: University of Pennsylvania Press.

Knappett, C. & Malafouris, L. (Eds.). (2008). *Material Agency: Towards a Non-Anthropocentric Approach.* New York: Springer.

Kockelman, P. (2006). Residence in the world: Affordances, instruments, actions, roles, and identities. *Semiotica, 162,* 19–71.

Kockelman, P. (2012). *Agent, Person, Subject, Self.* New York: Oxford University Press.

Kohfeldt, D., Bowen, A. R., & Langhout, R. D. (2016). "They think kids are stupid": yPAR and confrontations with institutionalized power as context for children's identity work. *Revista Puertorriqueña de Psicología, 27*(2), 276–291.

Kozulin, A. (1986). Vygotsky in Context. In L. S. Vygotsky (Ed.), *Thought and Language* (rev. ed.). Cambridge, MA: MIT Press.

Kozulin, A. (1990). *Vygotsky's Psychology.* Cambridge, MA: Harvard University Press.

Langhout, R. D. & Thomas, E. (2010). Imagining participatory action research in collaboration with children: An introduction. *American Journal of Community Psychology, 46*(1–2), 60–66.

LCHC (Laboratory of Comparative Human Cognition). (2010). Cultural-historical activity theory. In P. Peterson, R. Tierney, E. Baker, & B. McGaw (Eds.), *International Encyclopedia of Education* (Vol. 6, pp. 360–366). Kidlington: Academic Press.

Leander, K. M. (2002). Polycontextual construction zones: Mapping the expansion of schooled space and identity. *Mind, Culture, and Activity, 9*(3), 211–237.

Lemke, J. L. (2000). Across the scales of time: Artifacts, activities and meanings in ecosocial systems. *Mind, Culture, and Activity, 7*(4), 273–290.

Leont'ev, A. N. (1981). The problem of activity in psychology. In J. V. Wertsch (Ed.), *The Concept of Activity in Soviet Psychology.* Armonk, NY: M.E. Sharpe.

Lodewyk, K. R., Winne, P. H., & Jamieson-Noel, D. L. (2009). Implications of task structure on self-regulated learning and achievement. *Educational Psychology, 29*(1), 1–25.

Luria, A. R. (1928). The problem of the cultural development of the child. *Journal of Genetic Psychology, 35*(4), 493–506.

Martinek, D., Hofmann, F., & Kipman, U. (2016). Academic self-regulation as a function of age: The mediating role of autonomy support and differentiation in school. *Social Psychology of Education, 19*(4), 729–748.

Mead, G. H. (1934/1962). *Mind, Self and Society.* Chicago: University of Chicago Press.

Meyer, D. & Turner, J. (2006). Re-conceptualizing emotions and motivation to learn in classroom contexts. *Educational Psychology Review, 18*(4), 377–390.

Miller, P. & Goodnow, J. (1995). Cultural practices: Toward an integration of culture and development. In J. Goodnow, P. Miller, & F. Kessel (Eds.), *New Directions for Child Development* (Vol. 67, pp. 5–16). San Francisco: Jossey-Bass.

Ochs, E. (1990). Indexicality and socialization. In J. Stigler & R. A. Schweder (Eds.), *Cultural psychology: Essays on Comparative Human Development* (pp. 287–308). Cambridge: Cambridge University Press.

Ochs, E. (1993). Constructing social identity: A language socialization perspective. *Research on Language and Social Interaction, 26*(3), 287–306.

Ochs, E. (1996). Linguistic resources for socializing humanity. In J. J. Gumperz & S. C. Levinson (Eds.), *Rethinking Linguistic Relativity* (pp. 407–437). Cambridge: Cambridge University Press.

Panadero, E. (2017). A review of self-regulated learning: Six models and four directions for research. *Frontiers in Psychology, 8*, 1–28.

Panadero, E. & Järvelä, S. (2015). Socially shared regulation of learning: A review. *European Psychologist, 20*(3), 190–203.

Peirce, C. S. (1934). *Collected Papers of Charles Sanders Peirce*. Cambridge, MA: Harvard University Press.

Precht, K. (2003). Stance moods in spoken English: Evidentiality and affect in British and American conversation. *Text, 23*(2), 239–257.

Rief, S. (2007). Strategies to improve self-regulation. In S. Goldstein (Ed.), *Understanding and Managing Children's Classroom Behavior: Creating Sustainable, Resilient Classrooms* (pp. 322–360). Hoboken, NJ: John Wiley & Sons.

Rogoff, B. (1990). *Apprenticeship in Thinking: Cognitive Development in Social Context*. New York: Oxford University Press.

Rommetveit, R. (1979). On the architecture of intersubjectivity. In R. Rommetveit & R. M. Blakar (Eds.), *Studies of Language, Thought, and Verbal Communication* (pp. 93–108). London: Academic Press.

Rommetveit, R. (1984). The role of language in the creation and transmission of social representations. In R. Farr & S. Moscovici (Eds.), *Social Representations* (pp. 331–359). Cambridge: Cambridge University Press.

Sacks, H., Schegloff, E. A., & Jefferson, G. A. (1974). A simplest systematics for the organization of turn-taking in conversation. *Language, 50*(4), 693–735.

Sarason, S. (1981). *Psychology Misdirected*. New York: Free Press.

Sawyer, R. K. (2005). *Social Emergence: Societies as Complex Systems*. Cambridge: Cambridge University Press.

Scherer, K. R. (2000). Psychological models of emotion. In J. Borod (Ed.), *The Neuropsychology of Emotions* (pp. 137–162). New York: Oxford University Press.

Schieffelin, B. B. (1996). Creating evidence. In E. Ochs, E. A. Schegloff, & S. A. Thompson (Eds.), *Interaction and Grammar* (pp. 435–460). New York: Cambridge University Press.

Schunk, D. H. & Zimmerman, B. J. (2006). Competence and control beliefs: Distinguishing the means and ends. In P. A. Alexander & P. H. Winne (Eds.), *Handbook of Educational Psychology* (2nd ed., pp. 349–367). New York: Routledge.

Scribner, S. & Cole, M. (1981). *The Psychology of Literacy*. Cambridge, MA: Harvard University Press.

Shotter, J. (1993). Vygotsky: The social negotiation of semiotic mediation. *New Ideas in Psychology*, *11*(1), 61–75.

Shotter, J. (2014). Agential realism, social constructionism, and our living relations to our surroundings: Sensing similarities rather than seeing patterns. *Theory & Psychology*, *24*(3), 305–325.

Shotter, J. (2016). *Speaking Actually: Towards a New 'Fluid' Common-Sense Understanding of Relational Becomings*. Farnhill, UK: Everything Is Connected Press.

Shweder, R. A. (1991). *Thinking Through Cultures*. Cambridge, MA: Harvard University Press.

Silver, D. (2011). The moodiness of action. *Sociological Theory*, *29*(3), 199–222.

Smagorinsky, P. (2018). Deconflating the ZPD and instructional scaffolding: Retranslating and reconceiving the zone of proximal development as the zone of next development. *Learning, Culture, and Social Interaction*, *16*, 70–75.

Stone, L. D. (1996). The social construction of mathematical knowledge: Presented problems in mathematics classrooms. *Issues in Applied Linguistics*, *7*(1), 119–133.

Stone, L. D. & Gutierrez, K. D. (2007). Problem articulation and the processes of assistance: An activity theoretic view of mediation in game play. *International Journal of Education Research*, *46*(1–2), 43–56.

Stone, L. D. & Hart, T. (2002). Identities of competency and literacy learning. Research article. Child Development. California State University.

Stone, L. D. & Hart, T. (2007). Semiotic mediation in literacy practices: Private speech in context. *Language in Action: Vygotsky and Leontevian Legacy Today* (pp. 280–305).

Stone, L. D., Kerrick, M., & Stoeckl, R. (2013). Practical-moral knowledge: The social organization of regulatory processes in academic settings. *Mind, Culture, and Activity*, *20*(4), 372–392.

Stone, L. D. & Thompson, G. A. (2014). Classroom mood and the dance of stance: The role of affective and epistemic stancetaking in the development of a classroom mood. *Learning, Culture, and Social Interaction*, *3*(4), 309–322.

Stone, L. D., Underwood, C., & Hotchkiss, J. (2012). The relational habitus: Intersubjective processes in learning settings. *Human Development*, *55*(2), 65–91.

Thompson, G. (2016). Temporality, stance ownership, and the constitution of subjectivity. *Language and Communication*, *46*, 30–41.

Thompson, G. & Dori-Hacohen, G. (2012). Framing selves in interactional practice. *Electronic Journal of Communication*, *22*(3/4), 1–26.

Throop, C. J. (2014). Moral moods. *Ethos*, *42*(1), 65–83.

Tomasello, M. (2000). Culture and cognitive development. *Current Directions in Psychological Science*, *9*(2), 37–40.

Valsiner, J. (2001). Process structure of semiotic mediation in human development. *Human Development*, *44*(2), 84–97.

Vygotsky, L. (1935). The problem of the environment. In R. van Der Veer & J. Valsiner (Eds.), *The Vygotsky Reader*. Cambridge, MA: Blackwell.

Vygotsky, L. (1971). *The Psychology of Art*. Cambridge, MA: MIT Press.

Vygotsky, L. S. (1929). The problem of the cultural development of the child. *Journal of Genetic Psychology, 36*(3), 415–434.

Vygotsky, L. S. (1934/1986). *Thought and Language*. Cambridge, MA: MIT Press.

Vygotsky, L. S. (1934/1987). *Thinking and Speech: The Collected Works of Lev Vygotsky* (Vol. 1). New York: Plenum Press.

Vygotsky, L. S. (1966). Genesis of the higher mental functions. In A. R. Luria & A. Smirnoff (Eds.), *Psychological Research in the USSR* (Vol. 1). Moscow: Progress Publishers.

Vygotsky, L. S. (1978). *Mind and Society*. Cambridge, MA: Harvard University Press.

Vygotsky, L. S. (1981). The genesis of higher mental functions. In J. V. Wertsch (Ed.), *The Concept of Activity in Soviet Psychology* (pp. 144–188). Armonk, NY: M.E. Sharpe.

Vygotsky, L. S. (1987). Conclusion. Further research: Development of personality and world view in the child (M. Hall, Trans.). In R. W. Rieber (Ed.), *The Collected Works of L.S. Vygotsky. Volume 4: The History of the Development of Higher Mental Functions* (241–251). Springer Science+Business Media, New York.

Vygotsky, L. S. (1993). *The Collected Works of L.S. Vygotsky*, Vol. 2 (J. Know & C. Stevens, Trans.). New York: Plenum Press.

Wagner, D. & Herbel-Eisenmann, B. (2008). "Just don't": The suppression and invitation of dialogue in the mathematics classroom. *Educational Studies in Mathematics, 67*(2), 143–157.

Wenger, E. (1998). *Communities of Practice: Learning, Meanings, and Identity*. New York: Cambridge University Press.

Wertsch, J. V. (1985a). The semiotic mediation of mental life: L.S. Vygotsky and M.M. Bakhtin. In E. Mertz & R. J. Parmentier (Eds.), *Semiotic Mediation: Sociocultural and Psychological Perspectives* (pp. 49–71). Orlando, FL: Academic Press.

Wertsch, J. V. (1985b). *Vygotsky and the Social Formation of Mind*. Cambridge, MA: Harvard University Press.

Wertsch, J. V. (1991). *Voices of the Mind*. Cambridge, MA: Harvard University Press.

Wertsch, J. V. (1998). *Mind as Action*. New York: Oxford University Press.

Whipple, M. (2005). The Dewey-Lippmann debate today: Communication distortions, reflective agency, and participatory democracy. *Sociological Theory, 23* (2), 156–178.

Wittgenstein, L. (1981). *Zettel* (2nd ed.). Oxford: Blackwell.

Wood, D., Bruner, J., & Ross, G. (1976). The role of tutoring in problem solving. *Journal of Child Psychology and Psychiatry*, 17, 89–100.

Wootson, C. R. (2018). Laura Ingraham mocked Parkland survivor David Hogg over college rejections. Now he's headed to Harvard. *Washington Post*,

December 22. www.washingtonpost.com/education/2018/12/22/laura-ingraham-taunted-david-hogg-over-collecge-rejections-he-just-said-he-got-into-harvard/?utm_term=.38658fbe92c

Zheng, L. (2016). The effectiveness of self-regulated learning scaffolds on academic performance in computer-based learning environments: A meta-analysis. *Asia Pacific Education Review, 17*(2), 187–202.

Index

activity, 14
affect, 87
affective stance, 75, 76, 82, 86, 92, 93, 95, 96, 97, 98, 99, 100, 101, 102, 103, 113
affordance, 16, 104, 109, 110
agency, 8, 11, 40, 49, 50, 65, 109, 113
agent, 19, 20
agential activity, 12, 16, 18, 108, 109, 112
agential learners, 16, 29, 110
artifact, 5
  concrete, 17
  ideational, 17
  material, 13, 17
  symbolic, 13, 17

Barad, Karen, 1, 8
behavioral regulation, 2, 3, 4, 5, 7, 8, 9, 10, 11, 13, 14, 16, 17, 18, 26, 27, 28, 29, 31, 32, 33, 34, 37, 38, 39, 49, 51, 55, 68, 72, 73, 76, 86, 88, 93, 97, 107, 108, 109, 110, 111, 112, 113
Blumer, Herbert, 38
Bourdieu, Pierre, 2, 18, 107
Bruner, Jerome, 37

CHAT, 9, 12, 13, 18, 19, 21, 23, 27, 53, 110
Cohen, Jennifer, 71
Cole, Michael, 2, 4, 12, 13, 14, 21, 23, 27, 38, 45, 91, 107
collaborative agents, 62, 80, 99
collaborative problem-solving mood, 95, 96, 99, 102, 104
collective epistemic stance, 98
collective problem-solving mood, 100
community ethos, 10, 64, 77
constraint, 16, 40, 109, 110
context creating, 1, 113
context using, 1, 113
contextual mood, 10, 18, 87, 88, 89, 91, 93, 95, 96, 104, 105, 106, 108, 112, 113
contextual resource, 51, 86

co-regulation, 3, 28, 41, 43, 44, 46, 48, 49, 52, 59, 63, 65, 67, 68, 69, 81, 84, 95, 99, 100, 102
cultural and semiotic resources, 2
cultural artifacts, 1, 13, 19, 20
cultural condition of social life, 33
cultural habit, 13
cultural practices, 7, 9, 12, 14, 17, 18, 23
  cooking, 7
  learning, 7, 8, 10
cultural psychology, 12
cultural relatedness, 33
cultural resources, 13, 27, 31
cultural selection mechanism, 21
cultural-historical activity theory, 9, 12

Dewey, John, 1, 18, 107, 113
dialogic context, 76, 92
dialogic identity, 86
Du Bois, John W., 74, 92
Duranti, Alessandro, 33, 40
dyadic talk, 33

ecological, 8, 9, 12, 14, 19, 24, 31, 34, 39, 50, 110
elementary psychological functions, 19, 27
emotion, 87, 90
emotional experience, 88, 91
Engeström, Yrjö, 2, 4, 19, 23, 24, 107
epistemic stance, 75, 76, 78, 79, 82, 84, 85, 86, 92, 93, 95, 96, 97, 98, 99, 100, 101, 102, 103, 104, 113
event, 14, 18, 21, 23, 24, 27, 32, 36, 43, 59, 63, 64, 67, 90, 92, 93
explicit identity, 84
explicit social identity, 73

feelings, 87
first-generation activity theory, 23
first-generation mediational triangle, 21
Flynn, Pierce, J., 109